STRAIGHT
TALK
ON YOUR
MONEY

STRAIGHT
TALK
ON YOUR
MONEY

**The Biggest Financial
Myths and Mistakes . . .
and How to Avoid Them**

DOUG HOYES, CA, CPA

MILNER &
ASSOCIATES INC
· EDITING · PUBLISHING · COMMUNICATIONS · CONSULTING

Library and Archives Canada Cataloguing in Publication
Hoyes, Doug, author
    Straight talk on your money : the biggest financial myths and
    mistakes... and how to avoid them / Doug Hoyes.

Issued in print and electronic formats.
ISBN 978-1-988344-03-4 (softcover).—ISBN 978-1-988344-04-1 (HTML)

    1. Finance, Personal. 2. Financial literacy. I. Title.

HG179.H694 2017   332.024   C2017-902223-7
                                            C2017-902224-5

Production Credits
Editor and project manager: Karen Milner
Copy editor: Lindsay Humphreys
Interior design and typesetting: Adrian So, AdrianSoDesign.com
Cover design: Adrian So, AdrianSoDesign.com
Printer: Friesens

Published by Milner & Associates Inc.
www.milnerassociates.ca

Printed in Canada
10 9 8 7 6 5 4 3 2 1

For the Marcels of the world

CONTENTS

PREFACE

In high school, I worked at the local hardware store on Saturdays and during the summer. I loved that job. The owner, Marcel, was a great guy. He let me drive his old Mustang home for lunch. He always wanted to own a hardware store, so when the opportunity arose, he quit his job, invested his life savings, and spent seventy hours a week on the floor, helping customers.

One day I got home late from school, and my father said he wanted to speak to me. Marcel had stopped by the house an hour before. He told my father the bad news.

The bank had called their loan.

The store was bankrupt.

I couldn't believe it. What happened?

The conventional wisdom in a retail store is easy to understand: if the item a customer wants is out of stock, they can't buy it, so have lots of inventory. The more you buy, the cheaper the per unit price. Borrow from the bank to fund operations, and use that leverage to make a profit.

Marcel thought he was doing the right thing by following the conventional wisdom; he worked hard, did his best, and now he was out of business, and I was unemployed.

After getting over the initial shock, I thought back over the last few months, and I realized that the warning signs were obvious. The store was in trouble. There was too much debt. Marcel had borrowed from the bank to grow inventory, and when sales were slow, he couldn't repay the bank.

Debt killed the store.

We were done.

I was just a seventeen-year-old kid, but that's when I decided I would learn how money worked, so that I could spot the warning signs of impending financial catastrophe and direct people out of harm's way.

I graduated from university with a Commerce and Economics specialist degree. I went to work as an auditor for KPMG, but soon realized that certifying that the balance sheet from six months ago was mathematically accurate was not helping people spot the warning signs of impending financial catastrophe. I transferred from auditing to the financial advisory services group, and started working with companies in financial trouble. I even helped a well-known retail store avoid bankruptcy (and go on to a very profitable twenty-year run), but helping companies meant I helped only a few companies a year.

And most of the time it wasn't the companies I was helping; it was the banks who loaned them money and wanted to recover as much as they could. Completing a successful receivership on behalf of a bank was financially lucrative, but not particularly satisfying.

So, in 1999, Ted Michalos and I opened the doors on our new firm, Hoyes, Michalos & Associates Inc., and since then I have focused on helping people deal with debt.

I can now spot impending financial disaster. Over the last two decades I've noticed that most of my clients thought they were doing the right thing. They weren't buying inventory, but they were using debt to leverage themselves into a bigger car or house, because that's what conventional wisdom says you should do. The financial advice that people get from parents, friends, and even from the financial industry itself, is often accepted as truth, handed down from person to person with no further thought. However, much of this generally accepted advice is built on myths about money rather than the facts. And basing financial decisions on myths or emotion instead of the facts of a particular situation can lead to serious, sometimes even disastrous, mistakes and consequences.

This book is a collection of the most common myths my clients have followed, all of which caused massive financial trouble.

This book shows you how to spot those myths, so you can avoid them and improve your chances of financial success.

It's too late for Marcel.

It's not too late for you.

[Introduction]

FOLLOWING THE CROWD CAUSES BAD DECISIONS

*Whenever you find yourself on the side of the majority,
it's time to pause and reflect.*

Mark Twain

The premise of this book is simple: Most of the financial mistakes people make are a result of following conventional wisdom—the generally accepted advice about money that we encounter from our parents, friends, and even advisors. The problem with following conventional wisdom is that it is often based on irrational emotions rather than on the specific facts of a situation, and therefore, conventional wisdom is often wrong.

Why do we take conventional wisdom at face value and not spend the time to consider all of the details and options carefully before making financial decisions? Two reasons: First, we have limited time and we can save time by following the crowd. Second, we are social creatures and we want to fit in; by following conventional wisdom, we assume we will make socially acceptable decisions.

Unfortunately, however, relying on conventional wisdom often leads to highly irrational decisions. You may disagree with that statement and believe you are rational, particularly when it comes to money—money is all about numbers, after all, and what could be more rational than a number? But as I will illustrate in this book, while you may think you are making a rational decision, in many cases you are making an emotional decision, and often it is one that is strongly influenced by conventional wisdom—this is the common underlying cause for the biggest and most common mistakes that people make with money.

I know this to be true because I see it every day in my work as a Chartered Professional Accountant (what we used to call a Chartered Accountant) and as a Licensed Insolvency Trustee (what we used to call a bankruptcy trustee). In my thirty-year career as a financial advisor, I have seen hundreds of intelligent, well-meaning people let their emotions get the better of them as they follow the conventional financial wisdom and get into serious money trouble.

I've seen people make the same mistakes again and again over the years, accepting the bill of goods they are sold by the big banks and the rest of the financial industry, or the conventional wisdom that gets handed down to them by friends, family, and society in general—wrong-headed beliefs about money that have become so widely accepted they have achieved the status of mythical truths.

Sadly, this blind adherence to unsupportable opinion invariably leads to making bad financial decisions. Even worse, in many cases, following the crowd without questioning assumptions and without giving some thought to one's own personal situation gets people into serious money trouble. Worst of all, consistently making bad financial decisions based on emotion rather than sound rationale often leads to the stress of serious money problems and, eventually, bankruptcy. I've seen this happen countless times and I've seen how much damage it can do to individuals and families.

I am here to tell you that, in many areas, everything you know about money is wrong. But don't despair, there is hope. This book examines twenty-two common myths about money, debunks them by shining the spotlight of truth and rational information on them, and gives you practical solutions that you can easily implement to avoid these common financial mistakes and improve your financial well-being. Each chapter presents simple, real-life examples of the financial catastrophes that are caused by following conventional wisdom, and then shows you the simple tweaks you can make to your approach to money management that will leave you debt-free and stress-free.

I just have one request for you, the reader of this book: read it with an open mind. There will be some points I make that you will disagree with; you may even laugh out loud at my stupidity and naïveté for advancing such a ridiculous position. I understand why you might feel that way, but all I ask is that you set your emotions aside and rationally consider the alternate viewpoint I'm sharing. As we progress through each chapter in this book, ask yourself one simple question: What are the facts? You don't have to trust my opinion; all you need to do is review the facts so that you can make an informed decision.

Throughout my career, I have personally advised well over ten thousand people in financial difficulty, and in my experience, it is not the thoughtful consideration of facts that is the cause of money problems, it's the opposite: financial problems are caused by blindly following conventional wisdom. The good news is that challenging conventional wisdom and thinking for yourself are easier to do than you might think, and doing so will dramatically increase your chances of achieving financial success.

Let's get started.

PART 1

CONVENTIONAL WISDOM'S FATAL FLAW

[Myth #1]

HUMANS ARE RATIONAL

Humans consider the facts and make rational decisions.

Conventional Wisdom

Humans Are Entirely Irrational

We all think we are rational human beings. We believe that when we have a decision to make, we analyze the facts and make a well-thought-out, rational decision. But we don't—and this includes you. You are like me and every other person on the planet. We think we make rational decisions but, in fact, our decisions are usually based on emotion, social pressures, and shortcuts. We are irrational.

Is it bad that we don't think through every decision we make? No, quite the contrary. You make thousands of decisions every day, so if you had to think through every single one, you would have "paralysis by analysis" and would never get anything done. Shortcuts, in most cases, greatly improve your decision-making efficiency. Allow me to illustrate.

You go to the store to do your weekly grocery shopping. There are twenty-two items you need to buy. One of the items is toothpaste. Toothpaste is important: if you don't brush your teeth you will have bad breath, bad teeth, and perhaps gum disease and other serious medical problems. This is why we all brush our teeth. So, what toothpaste will you buy on your trip to the store today?

A rational person would start by listing all of the attributes of toothpaste and rank them in order of importance. Your ranked list might look something like this:

1. Cavity prevention
2. Whitening
3. Breath freshening
4. Cost

My list might be different. I might rate cost as being more important than whitening power, but that's fine. We are both rational human beings considering our options.

Next, I (or any rational person) would make a list of all available types of toothpaste and do some research to determine which brands rank the highest for each attribute. Then it's a simple decision-making process: I would buy the type of toothpaste that ranks highest for the attributes I rank as most important. But is this what we really do? No. Let's analyze your decision-making process by taking a self-assessment test.

SELF-ASSESSMENT TEST #1

1. What brand of toothpaste do you currently use?
2. How long have you used that brand for?
3. Why did you start using that brand?
4. Does that brand meet your criteria for the best toothpaste?
5. Have you considered switching to a different brand?

This is a book, so obviously I can't see your answers to the self-assessment test, but let me guess at how you responded: You've used your current brand of toothpaste for many years. It may be the brand that your parents used or it may be the brand your spouse uses. You have not considered investigating new options to determine if there is a better brand for you, despite all of the recent advances in toothpaste technology.

You are stuck in the toothpaste past. If my guesses are correct, then your toothpaste-purchasing decision-making process is not rational and you are probably not using the best toothpaste for you.

Now, I realize that, regardless if it's not the best toothpaste for you, your brand choice will probably have no impact on your overall quality of life. And sure, I, too, may use my brand of toothpaste only because I've used it since childhood or because my spouse uses it, in which case I'm "following the crowd" in my toothpaste-buying preferences as well. But so what? This may be an irrational decision, but who cares?

The fact that you and I make irrational decisions in inconsequential areas of our lives, such as what toothpaste we use, is immaterial. But what about more important decisions? Are you completely rational when you are required to make a potentially life-altering decision?

Nope.

We humans are social creatures, so in most cases we want to conform to the behavior of our social group. We don't make waves. We don't rock the boat. We go with the flow. We go by the book. We follow the conventional wisdom as dictated by our social group. Even with important decisions, we are irrational.

But wait, you say, that's crazy talk! I'm my own person. I make my own decisions. I'm unique. I don't follow the crowd.

Yes, you do. Let me prove it with another self-assessment quiz.

SELF-ASSESSMENT TEST #2

1. What toothpaste do you use? (Oh wait, I already proved my point on this one. You follow the crowd.)

2. Of all of the places in the world, where do you live? Why?

3. What is your religion? Is it the same religion as your parents? Your friends?

4. What type of clothes do you wear? Are they similar to the style worn by your co-workers and friends?

5. What television shows do you watch? Do your friends watch similar shows?

6. Do you own a house, or do you rent? Why?

7. Do you drive a car to work or take public transit? Why?

Whatever your answers are to these questions, did you arrive at those particular decisions after considering all of the facts and making a rational choice? Or were your decisions influenced by those around you? Think about it.

You could live and work anywhere in the country, or perhaps anywhere in the world, but you probably live close to where you grew up. The typical American lives only eighteen miles from his or her mother,[1] and I suspect we follow a similar pattern in Canada. Are we all making a rational decision to stay close to home, or is it more likely that we choose to do so because that's what most people do?

As for your clothes, you no doubt wear the same style of clothing as your co-workers do. If you work in an office, it wouldn't be appropriate to wear workout clothes, so your work attire is a rational decision. But is it completely rational? Could you wear a more interesting tie or socks or shirt if you wanted to? Do you choose your wardrobe simply to fit in?

I suspect that if most of your friends rent an apartment and take public transit to work, you probably do as well. And when your friends start buying cars and houses, it is likely that you will as well.

---

1. *www.nytimes.com/interactive/2015/12/24/upshot/24up-family.html?_r=0*

Perhaps this is simply rational demographics; at certain stages of life, we make certain decisions. It's not easy to raise a family in a bachelor apartment, after all. Perhaps your decision to own or rent is purely rational. Or is it?

Have you followed the conventional wisdom, likely handed down to you by your parents, that the decision to buy a house is the most important financial decision you can make and that it's the foundation for your financial future? If so, it's not a rational decision; it's following the crowd.

We typically do not have complete information when making a decision. For example, we don't know what the real estate market will do in the future, which makes it impossible to make a completely informed decision about buying a house. So what do we do? We follow conventional wisdom, as told to us by our family, friends, and society at large.

Following conventional wisdom is a convenient shortcut. I buy the same toothpaste I always buy because it's not worth spending two hours re-analyzing all of the new toothpaste technology and available brands every time we need a new tube. It's not worth the time.

But what about decisions regarding money? Is it worth it to spend time thinking about debt, real estate, and budgeting? Or should you just follow the conventional wisdom and do what everyone else is doing? The answer is unequivocally yes—it is definitely worth it to invest some brain power on significant financial decisions, because there is so much more at risk when it comes to deciding about investing or managing money than there is when you spend two bucks on a tube of toothpaste.

Perhaps you should buy a house, perhaps not. But the first step in making that decision is to acknowledge that you are not rational; that you, and I, make decisions based on emotion and are often influenced by social norms. If we realize this, we can briefly and intentionally set our emotions aside so that we can consider the facts and make an informed decision.

Rationalizing Is Not
the Same as Being Rational

Think back to the last major purchase you made. Maybe it was a car. If it was a new car, you probably believe that you chose that particular make and model based on a rational evaluation of its features, such as gas mileage, safety, and performance—but nope. In reality, you bought that car for purely irrational reasons, most likely because it conforms to your view of yourself.

If you perceive yourself as a young, sporty, action-oriented person, for example, you will have bought a sports car (even though you may be sixty years old and, for you, sports are now only something you watch on TV). Perhaps you liked the color or shape of the car or the location of the cup holders. The location of the cup holders is a perfectly good criterion to use when purchasing a car, but that's not the reason you give for selecting this model. Your "gut" decided that you wanted this car, and then you rationalized your decision by stating that it gets good gas mileage.

You think the steps in making a decision are: first use reason, then make the decision. But in fact, the process is exactly the opposite for most people. Your gut makes a decision, for purely emotional reasons, and then you consciously find reasons to rationalize your decision.

I'm not criticizing you—this is how we all do it, and car salespeople know it. They don't say, "Let me list all of the factual features of this car." They say, "Let's go for a test drive." Then, while on the test drive, they say, "Imagine what it would be like driving this car to work every morning. *Feels* good, doesn't it?"

Salespeople appeal to your emotions, not your rational mind. And only once you have decided to buy the car do they list the facts so you can convince yourself into believing you've made a rational, informed, fact-based decision.

Cognitive Reflection and Decision-Making

In the Fall 2005 edition of the *Journal of Economic Perspectives*, Shane Frederick, who at the time was an assistant professor at MIT, published a paper titled "Cognitive Reflection and Decision Making."[1] In his paper, Frederick introduced a three-item Cognitive Reflection Test, designed to illustrate the distinction between two types of cognitive processes:

1. System 1 decisions: made quickly, with minimal conscious deliberation
2. System 2 decisions: made more slowly and with reflection

When you see a red light, you stop. That's a System 1 decision. No thought is required; you simply react. That's good, because since you encounter some of the same decisions many times a day, it would be very inefficient (and unsafe) if you had to go into deep contemplative thought in order to decide what to do at a traffic light.

If I asked you to solve a complicated math question (like what loan amortization period and interest rate is best for you), you wouldn't be able to make a snap decision in arriving at your answer; you would have to think through the problem slowly and deliberately. This is a System 2 decision.

The problem is, we often make snap decisions when more contemplation is required.

SELF-ASSESSMENT TEST #3

For fun, let's take Dr. Frederick's Cognitive Reflection Test, which has only three questions (write down your answers before proceeding to the correct answers and explanations that follow the test):

1. A bat and a ball cost $1.10 in total. The bat costs $1.00 more than the ball. How much does the ball cost? _____ cents

---

1. *http://pubs.aeaweb.org/doi/pdfplus/10.1257/089533005775196732*

2. If it takes five machines five minutes to make five widgets, how long would it take one hundred machines to make one hundred widgets? _____ minutes

3. In a lake, there is a patch of lily pads. Every day, the patch doubles in size. If it takes forty-eight days for the patch to cover the entire lake, how long would it take for the patch to cover half of the lake? _____ days

For the first question, your brain makes a System 1 decision and says, "That's easy: the bat costs $1.00, the ball costs 10 cents, for a total of $1.10. Done." The question has $1.00 in it, so your brain fills in the blank, adds 10 cents, and you're done. But you aren't done, because if the bat costs $1.00 and the ball costs 10 cents, the bat costs only 90 cents more than the ball, so that's the wrong answer. The correct answer is: the ball costs 5 cents, the bat costs $1.05, for a total of $1.10.

According to Dr. Frederick's paper, "In a study conducted at Princeton, which measured time preferences using both real and hypothetical rewards, those answering '10 cents' were found to be significantly less patient than those answering '5 cents.'"

We humans jump to conclusions, even when dollars and cents are involved. If the decision appears obvious, we often use our "System 1" gut instead of our "System 2" brain to make the correct decision. For example, what would you say is better: a monthly car payment of $511 or $718? Our gut says $511, but as we will learn in Chapter 6, paying $511 for seventy-two months works out to be more in total payments than payments of $718 over forty-eight months. So the lesson is: do the math using all of the facts, don't jump to the obvious conclusion. But this is difficult to do.

Let's move on to the second question: If it takes five machines five minutes to make five widgets, how long would it take one hundred machines to make one hundred widgets? Most people would guess one hundred minutes because that completes the obvious pattern and we humans like patterns. But the correct answer is five minutes, because we know that each machine takes five minutes to build a widget. So whether you have five machines or a hundred, the task of creating a widget will be completed in five minutes.

What about Dr. Frederick's lake with the patch of lily pads? Every day, the patch doubles in size, so if it takes forty-eight days for the patch to cover the entire lake, how long would it take for the patch to cover half of the lake? The obvious answer is twenty-four days. Makes sense, right? If it is fully covered in forty-eight days, you would think it would take half that time, twenty-four days, to cover half the lake. You would think that, but you would be wrong. Here's why: If the patch doubles in size each day, the lake would be half-covered on day forty-seven, and then would double in size on the last day to cover the entire lake. So the correct answer is forty-seven days.

If you are naturally a cognitively reflective person, that's good, because you probably took your time and answered all of these questions correctly. If you are an overly cognitively reflective person though, it probably takes you a long time to make a decision, which isn't good. The trick is to ponder when necessary and act quickly when required, and it's sometimes difficult to know the difference. The reality is that most of us are not cognitively reflective by nature.

Let's take another example. If you put $1,000 in an investment that will double in value in ten years, what will it be worth in nine years? If you guessed $500, you are incorrect. This is not a lily-pad-in-a-lake question, it's a different type of question, so you can't use System 1 to guess the answer. (The answer is $1,870, because the investment is earning 7.2 percent per year, which we know from the Rule of 72 and which we will discuss in more detail when we get to Myth #4, but I digress.)

With money, the answers are not always obvious. This is why we make mistakes. We are irrational humans. When you are sitting in a car dealership, you want to buy that car; you don't want to do math. When your financial advisor is selling you an investment, you're thinking about what you will do with the hoped-for profit; you aren't considering how the high management fees will reduce your returns, and you are probably not accurately assessing the risk.

With Just the Facts, We Can Be Rational

Okay, you get it—humans make irrational decisions. But, of course, this isn't *always* true. Sometimes we are rational, particularly if we don't have conventional wisdom or generally accepted knowledge to fall back on. For example, if you know absolutely nothing about the game of cricket and I give you all of the statistics for all of the players that have ever played in the English Cricket League and ask you to assemble a list of the top ten players of all time, you would probably do a decent job of compiling a list that can be supported by the facts.

You could look at batting averages and fielding percentages and games played and championships won and other numbers, and make an honest evaluation of the best players of all time. Your evaluation would be honest and rational because you have no emotional connection to the English Cricket League, so you could make a purely rational evaluation based on the facts. I know this to be true because there is no such thing as the English Cricket League. I just made it up, because I, perhaps like you, know nothing about cricket.

Whenever you have an emotional interest in a decision, however, emotion takes over, and you are less likely to make a decision based on facts. For instance, take this question: Who is the best hockey player of all time? There are objective standards that you could use to make the determination, but if you ask a Canadian who has watched hockey for his or her entire life, you will more than likely get an answer based on emotion, not fact.

I believe the correct answer is Bobby Orr because he was my favorite player growing up and he scored the series-winning goal to clinch the 1970 Stanley Cup and he did it again in 1972, and his team, the Boston Bruins, won that year too.

See what I did there? I used my emotions to determine the answer. If you asked me, I would tell you that picking Bobby Orr as the best player of all time is based on a rational evaluation of the statistics (he does have the record for the most points ever by a defenseman), but, in truth, my emotions made the decision and then I used rational arguments, after the fact, to support my decision.

When we have an emotional attachment to a decision, we use emotions to make that decision, and it is therefore not a rational one. We make small decisions (like toothpaste buying) based on short-cuts that are not completely rational, and we make big decisions (like buying a car) entirely based on emotion (even though we will justify them, after the fact, with a recitation of the rational considerations we pretend we used to arrive at our car-buying decision).

We Follow Our Emotions to Fit In

But what influences the emotions on which we base our decisions? Why don't we acknowledge that we are emotional beings and make a conscious decision to make only those decisions that can be supported by facts and not by emotions? It's because we are social beings.

If you lived alone on an island and never encountered another human being, your decisions would be primarily rational and based on facts; your very survival would depend on it. You, however, do not live on an island. You interact with other people all day, every day. You are a social being. To survive, both emotionally and physically, you require the support of other people. For instance, how long could you survive at your job if you were constantly fighting with your co-workers? Not long. Your working environment is much more pleasant if you get along with your colleagues. The same is true of your daily interactions with family, friends, and acquaintances. Harmony is much more pleasant than conflict.

This is why, when you're faced with a decision, while you want to make the correct one based on facts, often it is more important that you make your decision based on the social implications of that decision. We make decisions to please our family, even when that decision is not the rational decision to make based on the facts. We make decisions to fit in with the group because we want to belong. We don't want to be ostracized.

If all of your friends rent apartments, for example, it is likely that you will also rent an apartment. Once your friends start buying condos or houses, it is likely that you will do the same. Is it because buying a house is the correct financial decision for you? Perhaps, but it is even more likely that you are buying a house to fit in with your social group.

This phenomenon could be described as peer pressure, but it's more than that. Peer pressure has a negative connotation: being coerced into taking an action you otherwise would not take. I'm describing a phenomenon you perceive as positive, not negative. Your friends are doing it, so you believe it must be the correct decision.

Because we want to fit in, we will often make a decision that we believe will make the right impression on our friends, even if the facts would support an alternate decision. If all of your friends drive a car to work, do you want to be the only one who takes the bus? If all of your friends are buying houses, do you want to be the only one who rents?

Conventional wisdom is the "wisdom of crowds." If all of your friends think it's a good idea to buy a house because they believe that house prices will go up, then the conventional wisdom among your circle of friends is that house prices will go up, and so you buy a house to follow along. This is one reason why conventional wisdom is often wrong. Your friends are not real estate experts. They are swayed by advertising and other influences, and it's likely that their decisions are not based entirely on rational facts, either.

Should you buy a house? In North American society, conventional wisdom says yes because, long term, it's a great investment. If the experts all agree on this, it must be the correct decision, right? Perhaps, but perhaps not. Real estate experts will tell you that flipping a house is a great investment; however, buying a house as a "quick flip" investment in Calgary in 2015 was not a great decision because the market dropped in 2016. In that situation, conventional wisdom was wrong.

Throughout history there have been many examples of conventional wisdom being wrong. Take Galileo Galilei, an Italian astronomer during the Renaissance who championed heliocentrism, the theory that the Earth revolves around the sun. Galileo was tried by the Roman Inquisition in 1615, found "vehemently suspect of heresy," and spent the final nine years of his life under house arrest. In 1615 everyone "knew," at an emotional level, that the Earth was the center of the universe (just look in the sky: the sun moves, not the Earth!), and no amount of rational thought or evidence to the contrary could convince them otherwise.

But as we all of course now know, conventional wisdom at the time was wrong, and the Earth is not the center of the universe. It was not until 1992 that Pope John Paul II finally expressed regret for how the Galileo affair was handled, and he apologized.

Bearing in mind that conventional wisdom can be wrong (and sometimes wrong for a long time), it can be dangerous or harmful to us if we fail to realize that our emotions may influence us to make an incorrect decision by following conventional wisdom. This is why we need to learn to be more rational and less impulsive; to be less inclined to go with the thinking that seems the most obvious, precisely because it is accepted as conventional wisdom.

This is of particular importance when it comes to making financial decisions because, as discussed earlier, those decisions can have such a huge impact on your life. There are no one-size-fits-all answers to financial questions, so we must each learn how to think them through in order to determine the best solution for ourselves in whatever particular situation we are in.

Practical Advice: Recognize that You Are an Irrational, Emotional Being

Look, I understand. You don't subscribe to the *Journal of Economic Perspectives*, and you have no interest in reading Dr. Shane Frederick's "Cognitive Reflection and Decision Making" paper. You simply want to make better financial decisions—good for you. So here's my advice.

The first step is to acknowledge that human beings are not rational and we all make decisions based on emotion. If we realize this, we can briefly set our emotions aside so that we can consider the facts and make an informed decision. When faced with a financial decision, it's okay to *start* by letting your "gut" be your guide. If your gut says, "Buy that car that says 'turbo' on the back," great. But before you *actually* buy that car, ask yourself the most important question: "Am I making a rational or an emotional decision?" This appears to be a simple question to answer, but it isn't. When you are under the control of your emotional gut, you are not aware that you are under the control of your emotional gut.

For instance, take the Dutch tulip craze that happened in the seventeenth century. At the peak of "tulip mania" in 1637, a single tulip bulb sold for more than ten times the annual income of a skilled craftsman. It was not rational to buy a tulip bulb at those prices, but the irrational expectation of ever-increasing profits overrode rational thought and everyone was buying tulip bulbs, because emotion trumps reason.

At the height of the dot-com stock market bubble in 2000, Internet companies with no earnings were selling for hundreds of times their *projected* profit. It was crazy, and those stocks subsequently crashed, but speculators' emotional guts ruled their rational brains, and they made catastrophically bad decisions.

The solution to this gut–brain problem is easy to say but difficult to implement: you must consciously acknowledge that you make emotional decisions, step back, consider the decision based on the rational facts, and only *then* make a decision. You must, because you are irrational.

[Myth #2]

IT'S YOUR FAULT

We are the architects of our own lives.
We make our own luck.

Conventional Wisdom

Life Happens

In the area of personal finance, conventional wisdom is clear: You are responsible for your own situation. If you have too much debt, it's because you spent too much. If you can't find a good job, it's because you aren't looking hard enough. If you won't retire by age fifty, it's because you didn't save enough and you didn't invest wisely.

Your money problems are your fault. That's the conventional wisdom. Which brings me to the story of Sarah.

Sarah was raised by a single mother, so at an early age she learned the value of hard work. She started babysitting the neighborhood kids when she turned thirteen, and by age sixteen she had two part-time jobs, working in a store (after school) and a restaurant (on weekends).

Sarah saved enough money that she was able to pay for a good portion of her university education when the time came, and when she graduated (with honors) she was happy to have only $10,000 in student loan debt, which was far less debt than her peers.

The year she graduated from university was a tough year. The economy was in a recession. Not able to find a job in her field, Sarah went back to working two jobs, in retail and food service, and she earned only minimum wage.

Two years after graduating, Sarah got a job as an intern in her field, but it was an unpaid internship, so she continued working her weekend job to survive. Once she was able to put the internship experience on her résumé, Sarah finally found an entry-level position in her field.

Unfortunately though, the job required her to have a car and, with minimal credit history, Sarah's only option was to finance a used car through a high-interest lender. She used her credit card to buy some clothes for work.

She did great at her job, but now that she was working she was required to start making payments on her student loan and, with her car loan and credit card payments as well, Sarah was only able to make the minimum payments.

Then, one morning on the way to work, Sarah was hit by a drunk driver. She broke her arm and leg, her car was destroyed, and she spent six weeks in hospital recovering. Her car insurance paid her the replacement value of her used car, which was barely enough to repay the existing loan. Health insurance covered her stay in the hospital, but her sick benefits didn't start until she was off work for six weeks, so she had no choice but to use her credit card to pay her rent and car insurance in the meantime.

Sarah was lucky. She made a speedy recovery and was back to work three months after the accident. Her employer was very accommodating, not only by holding her job for her until she returned, but by shifting her work responsibilities so she could continue her physiotherapy. But now her student loan and credit card were in arrears, so in order to replace her car with another used car, she had to take out a car loan with a higher interest rate. Sarah realized that, on her current income, the best she could hope for would be to make her minimum payment, and only if her income were to increase would she be able to think about saving.

Sarah was fortunate that she was able to return to work relatively quickly, she didn't have a spouse or child to support, and she didn't have a big mortgage to worry about it. Her situation could have been much worse. But, even as one of the lucky ones, Sarah, a hard worker and prudent saver, was still stuck with a lot of debt and no prospects to get out of debt anytime soon.

So now, dear reader, I ask you to consider these questions:

Was Sarah's difficult financial situation her fault?

What should Sarah have done differently?

What different actions could Sarah have taken to avoid her dire financial circumstances?

Perhaps instead of going to university, she should have continued to work at her minimum-wage jobs. Had she done that, she would not have had to get a student loan and, with hard work, she presumably would advance to a job that would pay more than minimum wage. Perhaps she should not have been driving to work on a road on which a drunk driver was also driving.

Or perhaps there wasn't anything Sarah could have done to avoid her current circumstances. She did everything right, and she still ended up in debt. It's not her fault.

The Stunning Realization

It's true: Sarah's financial problems are not her fault. That stunning realization goes against the conventional wisdom that says we make our own luck. There are a number of personal finance "experts," many of whom are American and have their own radio or television shows and write lots of books, who would disagree with the statement that Sarah's money worries are not her own fault. They would argue that "into each life some rain must fall" but that, with a good work ethic and frugal lifestyle, Sarah can get back on track.

Let's test that hypothesis by doing the math. Let's assume that Sarah's take-home pay is $2,500 per month, and let's assume that her rent, food, transportation, and other basic living expenses are also $2,500 per month. Here's the math question: How much can Sarah afford each month to pay down her credit card and student loan debt? I'll wait while you get out your calculator to perform this complicated computation.

Of course, you don't need a calculator to figure this out. The answer is obvious, even to those who are math-challenged. Despite living a prudent and frugal lifestyle, Sarah has no extra money to devote to debt repayment or savings. None.

So there you have the fallacy of the hypothesis that getting into debt is all your own fault and you just have to work harder to make ends meet. Sometimes the ends don't meet.

Using a Stacked Example to Prove the Point

But wait, you say. There is no Sarah. It's a made-up story. There was no hard-working person who just happened to encounter some bad luck. There are lots of stories of people who "pull themselves up by their bootstraps" and do great.

That is true. You can use anecdotal evidence to "prove" either side of the proposition. There are people, like Sarah, who worked hard and did not immediately succeed, just as there are people, like Bill Gates, who worked hard and did succeed. This is why we must acknowledge that circumstance (or luck, either good or bad), plays a part in our financial success or failure.

Let me be clear: there are indeed people who bring dire financial circumstances on themselves; they don't work hard or they live far beyond their means; they understand the ramifications of their actions, and yet they deliberately and knowingly do the wrong thing. I know, I've met them. But, in my experience, the vast majority of people who are in financial difficulty did not arrive at that state solely as a result of their own actions. Life happens. Sometimes circumstances simply work against our best intentions and plans. (Of course though, if you're a financial advice guru—selling books, DVDs, workbooks, courses, and Internet webinars—"it's not your fault" does not sell. Telling people that some circumstances are beyond their control does not make for a two-day weekend seminar.)

Some circumstances are your fault. If you jump off your roof and break your leg, your broken leg is your fault. If the other driver runs a red light and you break your leg in the resulting car accident, your broken leg is not your fault. Your leg is broken in either scenario, but broken legs are not automatically the fault of the leg-owner. Does it matter how you got your broken leg? For the purposes of repairing your broken leg, no, it doesn't matter how you broke it, but understanding what happened to cause the injury can help you avoid that mistake in the future.

If your problems are your fault, what matters is what steps you take to prevent them from occurring again in the future. If you didn't cause your problems, all the advice in the world will not prevent those problems from re-occurring.

The Folly of the Financial Gurus' Advice

I'm not opposed to the basic message that we should work hard and save money. In fact, I agree with that message. I also agree that going for an hour-long walk each day is good exercise and can lead to very significant health benefits—unless you have a broken leg, in which case trying to walk for an hour a day, with or without a cast, is a very bad idea.

That's why you can't simply accept the message that your financial problems are your fault and then set about solving them using conventional methods. Sarah worked hard, but with an interruption in income and the resulting increase in her debt, hard work alone was not sufficient to prevent financial problems.

If all of my friends can run a five-kilometer race in thirty minutes and it takes me an hour, am I out of shape? Do I simply need to train harder to improve my time? Perhaps—unless my problem is that I have a broken leg. Then all of the training in the world won't help until my leg heals. Similarly, if you have a massive amount of debt, trying to follow one widely known piece of conventional wisdom and set aside 10 percent of your income in a savings plan is pointless. Saving for retirement is not a priority when your wages are about to be garnisheed.

To continue the metaphor, you have to start by healing your broken leg (paying down your debt), then you can progress to walking (starting to save a little of each paycheck), and only then you can run (following a more aggressive plan to save for retirement).

Reasons Why Your Financial Woes May Not Be Your Fault

Based on a review of all of the people I've helped with debt problems over the years, I can easily list five common reasons why your money problems may not be entirely your fault.

1. Aggressive and Sophisticated Marketing

The big banks' financial statements show that they each spend many hundreds of millions of dollars on "communications" each year in the form of television and radio commercials and print and online advertising. But these aren't the most difficult types of advertising to resist as you can always avoid them if you want, by changing the channel, for example.

The most insidious form of advertising is direct solicitation. Have you ever received a "pre-approved" credit card application in the mail? Has your credit card company ever sent you a letter saying, "Congratulations, you didn't ask for it, but we've raised your credit limit!" Have you ever walked into a store and the friendly person at the front says, "Hey, if you apply for our credit card today, you'll get a free gift!" These are all common tactics of direct solicitation, and they are very difficult to resist.

Payday loan companies are equally sophisticated. They don't tell you, "Our annual interest rate is over 500 percent, so you may never be able to pay us off." Instead, they tell you, "It costs only $18 to borrow $100." That doesn't sound like much, but borrowing $18 on $100 every two weeks is the equivalent of an annual interest rate of 468 percent. It's hard to resist these sophisticated marketing tactics, and that's why if you do succumb to the temptation, it's not entirely your fault.

2. Job Loss or Underemployment

More than half of all of the bankruptcies and consumer proposals filed in Canada are caused primarily by a reduction in income, which in many cases is caused by job loss. But is it your fault if your company moved operations to Mexico or China? Probably not.

An equally common scenario is underemployment. Many companies offer medical benefits and a retirement plan to their full-time permanent employees. Doing this is expensive though, so companies today will hire two part-time employees instead of one full-time employee. The savings are significant for the company, but the cost to the employee is huge. Many employees must then have two or more part-time jobs and need to juggle their shifts to pick up enough hours to survive. If they get sick, forget it. With no benefits, they incur the costs. Is it their fault that they have to use debt to survive?

Temporary jobs are another risk factor for employees. To hire a full-time employee, an employer has to interview multiple candidates, pick the best one, and set him or her up on payroll. Then, if the employee proves months later not to be suitable for the job, the employer must terminate him or her and incur the financial costs of any severance and the costs to hire a replacement employee, including the time cost of going through the hiring process all over again.

That's why employers use temp agencies for clerical or manufacturing or service-industry employees. This way, they have an unlimited supply of employees and if someone doesn't work out the employer can terminate them, at no cost, and get another one tomorrow. No severance and no benefits.

I know of one large employer at which the majority of the workforce is composed of temporary employees on short-term contracts. I've met with many employees who have worked at that company for as much as seven years, off and on, but they are still contract employees with no benefits. They go through periods of unemployment until the next contract starts, during which time they use debt to survive. Is it their fault that they can't find a full-time, permanent job with benefits?

3. Illness

What would happen if you, like Sarah, were in a car accident? Or got injured at work? Or found out you had cancer and required six months of radiation and chemotherapy? Do you have enough money in the bank to cover your rent or mortgage and pay for food and medication and all of your other living costs for the six months you'd be off work?

Most people don't have six months' worth of cash just sitting there, so a medical problem can be financially ruinous. Is it your fault if you get sick or injured?

4. Divorce

One in seven insolvencies in Canada is caused, at least in part, by a relationship breakdown. More than a quarter of people filing bankruptcy are divorced or separated at the time they file.

We can debate whether or not it's your fault that you got divorced, but there is no debate over the financial implications of the break-up.

When you are living with a partner, together you have one bill to pay each month for each household bill: rent, hydro, gas, cable, and home phone. You may even be able to share a car. It's not true that two can live as cheaply as one, but it's close. When you separate, you must each now pay your own rent and all other living expenses. Your living costs may have doubled but, unfortunately, you now have only one income, and that's a recipe for financial problems: lower income, higher expenses.

In many cases, the process of separating is very expensive. You incur costs to move to a new place, and you need first and last month's rent as well as a security deposit for your utilities (if they are not included in your rent). If you don't have the cash on hand, you must borrow to start your new life. If a legal separation is required, you may need to hire a lawyer. If children are involved, the lawyer's bills can be significant, and that leads to more borrowing.

Could you survive a separation tomorrow? Do you have sufficient resources to start a new life? Many people don't, and it's not their fault.

5. Student Loans

More than 15 percent of all insolvent debtors in Canada had a student loan at the time they filed for bankruptcy or a consumer proposal.

When I went to university in the 1980s, tuition was low (around $1,000 per year), so a student could get a summer job, earning minimum wage, and make enough money to cover tuition and books. If your parents were able to cover your living expenses, you could complete a four-year program without the need to resort to student loans to fund your higher education.

Today, it's a different story. Tuition for a typical undergraduate program at a typical Canadian university starts at $6,000 per year, and a more specific program can easily have annual tuition costs of $10,000 or more. Add in the cost of living expenses plus books and other fees, and a year of post-secondary education can easily cost $20,000 or more. How many students can earn $20,000 at a summer job?

If you were a student today and could find a summer job that paid $12 per hour and you were able to work forty hours per week for sixteen weeks, you could gross $7,680, which of course would be less than that after taxes and other deductions. Even students who can also work eight hours per week throughout the school year at a part-time job would be fortunate to earn half of the cost of a typical university education. If your parents couldn't make up the difference, your only other option would be a student loan. Even if you were able to cover half of your costs, you'd graduate after four years with $40,000 in debt.

Would that student debt be your fault? Should you have skipped college or university and entered the workforce right out of high school? Perhaps, but without a post-secondary education it might be more difficult to find a well-paying job. For young people today there are no easy answers, and it's not their fault.

So Whose Fault Is It?

The purpose of this book is not to assign blame. If you want a quick answer, it's that money troubles are everyone's fault. It's my fault for borrowing too much, but it's also the government's fault for high taxes that make it difficult to save money and the bank's fault for aggressive lending practices that make it hard not to borrow.

But blame doesn't matter. The point is that many people today have debt and other financial problems that are not entirely their fault. The sooner we acknowledge this reality, the sooner we can start working on solutions—and solutions for the future are much more productive than playing the blame game for perceived past sins.

Practical Advice: Focus on the Positive

If you're the type of person who never worries about the past and is always looking forward, you would make a great baseball relief pitcher. You'd give up a home run to lose the game in the ninth inning today, but you'd be able to bounce back and pitch again tomorrow, totally unaffected by the past. If you're this kind of person, this chapter was not for you. This chapter was written for people who use their current circumstances to negatively influence their future.

Remember when you were learning to ride a bicycle? You fell down fifty-seven times in a row and were ready to give up. You cried when you cut and scraped yourself, blamed yourself for your lack of coordination, and felt bad because every other kid you knew was racing around the block without a care in the world. And then, one day, it clicked. But if you had focused on the fifty-seven "failures" and given up, you would never have learned to ride a bike. This is because the fifty-seven times you fell were not failures: they were necessary learning experiences. Experiencing what actions lead to a bicycle crash teaches you how to stay balanced on your bike.

I don't believe in failures; I believe in experiments and experiences. Thomas Edison had a thousand failures before he invented the light bulb. (I know he failed exactly one thousand times because I read it on the Internet.) I suspect that Mr. Edison viewed each of those thousand "failures" as an experiment. He knew that if he kept on trying he would eventually figure it out and that each failed experiment was actually a success because it brought him one step closer to his ultimate goal.

It's a question of mindset. What is your mindset? If light bulb experiment number 784 fails, would you become depressed at your long string of "failures," or would you say, "Great! I'm one step closer to success"? If you try to keep track of your spending but get behind on your record keeping, do you give up? Or do you use it as a learning experience? (For instance, I've learned that I don't love budgeting, so I need a different system for managing my money.) If you are currently in debt, do you get depressed and say to yourself, "I guess I'm just no good with money"? Is it your nature to assume your problems are your fault and, therefore, that there is nothing you can do to improve your situation? If so, that's the wrong approach.

Wherever you are now in your financial life, know this: you cannot change the past, but you can change the future. If you insist on blaming yourself for the events that led to your current predicament rather than learning how you can improve things going forward, you will stay stuck in your current situation. It's a negative mindset.

My practical advice is simple: Make a conscious decision to adopt a positive mindset. Don't view your failures as failures; view them as experiments. You can learn a lot from those experiments, and this will put you in a great position for the future because you will understand that you are not beholden to your past.

How do you move forward in the future? Do you need to find a guru to lead you to the path of enlightenment? No. Read on.

[Myth #3]

EXPERTS ARE EXPERTS

We live in a complex world. The average person can't possibly understand complex concepts like variable interest rates, compound interest, amortization schedules, options and derivatives. Expert advice is essential.

Conventional Wisdom

All Experts Are Biased

Play along with me here. Let's assume you acknowledge that you could do a better job of managing your money than you currently do. How do you get better? Who do you turn to? The answer is obvious, right? You turn to the experts.

Experts are easy to find. They write books. They appear on TV. They have their own YouTube channel and Twitter account, and they probably post pictures of what they had in their morning smoothie on Instagram. But just because someone has a large Twitter following does not, therefore, imply that you should follow their advice, because here's the deep dirty secret about experts: they are all *biased*.

All experts have their own agenda, and that agenda is not likely to be primarily focused on helping you.

Based on conventional wisdom, I'm an expert. The company I co-founded has a YouTube channel, with well over a hundred videos. I have appeared on television dozens of times and on the radio hundreds of times. You are now reading the book I wrote.

I also have lots of initials after my name:

- BA (Commerce and Economics Specialist, University of Toronto)
- CA (Chartered Accountant)
- CPA (Chartered Professional Accountant)
- CBV (Chartered Business Valuator)
- CIRP (Chartered Insolvency and Restructuring Professional)
- LIT (Licensed Insolvency Trustee)

With all of those letters after my name, I must be an expert. But should you believe everything I say because I have a lot of initials after my name? I worked very hard over many years to get all of those initials, so yes, I would *like* you to believe everything I tell you, but you would be crazy to believe everything I say. You would be reckless and foolish to follow any of my advice blindly. Why? Because all experts are biased, including me.

Follow the Money

Experts are biased, because experts, in most cases, are selling something. So before you trust any experts, figure out what they are selling. Follow the money.

Is your financial planner unbiased? Follow the money: how does he get paid? If your financial planner sells mutual funds, he gets paid by the mutual fund company. If you don't buy the company's mutual funds, your financial planner doesn't get paid. If Joe the financial planner sells mutual funds only from Big Mutual Fund Company, it is highly likely that Joe will recommend that you buy a mutual fund from Big Mutual Fund Company. Is that in your best interests, though? Would Joe be recommending a fund because it's the best fund for you, or would he do it because it's the only fund company that will pay Joe his commission, because Joe sells mutual funds only from that company? Even worse, is Joe recommending the fund that pays him the highest commission, and that's why he's recommending it?

I would ask my financial planner the following questions:

- How do you get paid?
- Do you sell mutual funds (or insurance, or mortgages, or whatever) from only one company or from many companies?
- Do you sell only one type of product (like mutual funds) or do you sell many types of investments (mutual funds, stocks, ETFs, bonds, etc.)?
- How do I know that you are giving me unbiased advice?

I am not suggesting financial planners who sell mutual funds are evil. They may be recommending an investment that is perfect for you and, if so, that's great. All I am suggesting is that you should understand their motives so that you can evaluate their advice with your eyes open.

If you go to the Ford dealership and ask the salesperson what type of car you should buy, there is a close to 100 percent chance that he will recommend a Ford. It may be a truck, or a large car, or a small car, but most likely it will be a Ford. What is the chance that of all of the different makes of car in the world, a vehicle made by Ford is the best one for you? I don't know, but I would guess that it's less than 100 percent. A different manufacturer may have other features that you need, or it may have a similar vehicle at a better price.

My point is not to criticize Fords. I'm not a car expert, but I assume Ford vehicles are similar to those of other car manufacturers and it is quite possible that the car the salesperson recommends will adequately suit your needs. My point is that you don't expect unbiased advice from a car salesperson. You expect the Ford dealer to sell you a Ford.

You also fully understand that when you walk into a car dealership and talk to the salesperson, you're talking to someone who wants to sell you a car. You are prepared for the salesperson to use all of the tricks in the book. He knows you make decisions based on emotion, so he will appeal to your emotions ("This car really suits you") and not your rational thought process ("Before we go for a test drive, let me list for you the eighty-seven features of this car"). Your guard is up. You are ready.

But for some reason, we think the world of money is different. When you sit down with your financial planner for your annual review and she asks you questions about your goals and helps you develop a financial plan, you don't view her as a salesperson. You view her as your advisor, someone who is working *for* you. Therefore, your guard is down. You don't perceive that you are talking to a salesperson. But ask yourself the key question: How does she get paid?

If she is charging you an hourly rate to prepare a financial plan, there's a good chance she's giving you relatively unbiased advice. If her advice doesn't work out, you won't hire her next year, so it is in her best interest to give you good advice. But what if the financial plan is "free"? How can your financial advisor spend three hours with you on a Wednesday evening creating a financial plan and then not charge you for it? How can she afford to work for free? She can't.

It is possible that she is creating the financial plan to show you that you need to save money for your retirement, and then she will recommend various mutual funds that she can sell you to accomplish that objective. It's possible that the "free" financial plan is simply the first step in the sales process.

Again, I am not saying that all financial planners are simply glorified salespeople. I suspect that the vast majority of them want you to be successful in your investments and, therefore, most of them are preparing a financial plan and giving you advice because they want to help you. That's great. But remember, they also want you to be successful with your investments because that's how *they* make money over the long term. No one cares about your financial well-being as much as you do so, at the very least, you should ask questions and be aware of your options, because all experts are biased in some way.

The Myth of the Unbiased Banker

What about the financial planner who works for a bank? Does a bank representative give you unbiased advice? Considering I have already said that all experts are biased, the answer to that question is easy: No, a banker does not give you unbiased advice.

In the "good old days," you went to the bank every week to deposit your pay. You always saw the same teller (I think her name was Myrtle). She knew you by name and she knew your family, so there was never a need to ask for identification. She deposited your money and processed your bill payments. Today though, bank tellers are an endangered species. Your pay is deposited electronically and you pay your bills online, so there is seldom a need to visit a "bricks and mortar" bank. When you do, you don't talk to a teller; you meet with a customer service representative, which is a fancy word for salesperson.

Try this experiment: go to a bank and open a bank account.

I tried it. I put on my best suit, walked into the branch where my company has banked for many years and where my company has a significant sum of money on deposit (in trust for our clients). I went to the information desk and told the young woman sitting there, "My company banks here and now I want to open a personal bank account."

She replied, "Great, Mr. Hoyes. I can book you an appointment with Mary. How's tomorrow afternoon at 2:00?"

I had two questions: where's Myrtle, and why can't I open the account now? The woman had no idea who Myrtle was, and she said that there are forms to fill out and procedures to follow, and how about 2:00 tomorrow?

So I went back at 2:00 the next day, with three forms of photo identification, and said I just wanted to open a savings account, nothing fancy. Mary, the very nice customer service representative I met with, explained about overdraft protection and credit cards and mutual funds and all of the other services the bank could offer. That's great, I told her, but I just want a simple bank account.

Mary was doing her job. Her job is to sell me the bank's services, and that's what she was doing. She was not suggesting overdraft protection in order to protect me; she was suggesting it because it's a profitable service for the bank. At the end of the day, Mary is a salesperson.

Let me once again belabor the obvious point: Someone like Mary may appear to be offering you unbiased advice as an "expert" working for the bank but, in fact, she is doing her job as a salesperson. Be forewarned: All of those bank services may be great, but they also have a cost, so being talked into services you don't need isn't helping you, it's helping the bank. The customer service representative you speak with may appear to be an expert, but that doesn't mean you should blindly follow what he or she is recommending.

The Tyranny of the Experts

The problem with some experts is that they don't encourage debate; they stifle it. They state an opinion, often because it is in their financial interest to do so (remember, follow the money), and if you voice an alternate opinion they say, "I'm an expert, you are not; so I'm right, end of debate."

For the remainder of this book, I will explain what the experts believe and I will tell you why what they say is often spectacularly bad advice. In many cases, you should actually do the exact opposite of what the experts tell you to do. Owning a house is often a horrible idea, for example; there is no such thing as good debt and bad debt;

you should not, in many cases, cash in investments to pay off debt; and so on and so on.

Don't let a tyrant do your thinking for you. If you ever hear an "expert" imply that "I'm an expert, you aren't," then you are about to receive bad advice. I guarantee it. Why? Because if my advice is genuinely good advice, I should be able to explain my position clearly and prove it with a rational argument, not by bullying.

This is my approach throughout this book: state my opinion and support it with logical reasoning. If I can't convince you, don't follow my advice. Question everything I say, because that's what you should do with anyone giving advice, particularly when it comes to financial matters.

When your stock broker says "buy this stock," don't blindly follow his advice. Ask for an explanation. Ask for numbers. Ask for details about what the company does, and why your broker thinks the recommended company's stock will increase in value. If your broker's company has a substantial position in the stock of the company being recommended, it is possible that he wants to sell you the stock so that he and his company can profit (again, follow the money). The stock may not be a good stock, and if you fall for the tyranny of the expert telling you it's a good deal without providing rational supporting evidence, you will make a bad decision.

I realize that we are not all experts in all areas of life. I'm not a doctor, so when my doctor gives me a diagnosis and provides suggestions for treatment, what should I do? The answer is simple, and it's the same answer that applies in all areas of life: Think. Did the doctor do a thorough examination of me and ask lots of questions, or did she jump to conclusions in making her diagnosis? Did she explain the various treatment options or just prescribe a drug (that may or may not be sold by the drug company that took the doctor out golfing yesterday). Use the Internet. Do your research. If the doctor's recommendation checks out, great, follow it. If not, go back and ask more questions or find another doctor. Doctors are not infallible.

Financial advisors are also not infallible. I am willing to acknowledge the possibility that everything I write in this book is wrong. I doubt that this is true, but it is possible. Like I told you earlier, just because I have many initials after my name and just because I've served as a financial advisor for thirty years doesn't mean that you should follow every word I write.

Practical Advice: Nobody Cares About Your Money as Much as You Do

Before automatically accepting any so-called expert's advice just because they have lots of initials after their name or have their own radio show or have written a lot of books, dig deeper. Their advice may be great, or it may follow conventional wisdom and be completely wrong for your situation. As with all things in life, *caveat emptor*: buyer beware.

You may encounter financial tyrants who attempt to impose their will on you, but you have a significant advantage over them and over every other expert: You are you, and you have a brain. You know your personal situation and your goals better than anyone else. And so you can consider all advice, do your own research, think, and make an informed decision. Remember: Follow the money, and don't fall for the tyranny of expertise.

PART 2
DEBT

[Myth #4]

GIVE CREDIT WHERE CREDIT IS DUE

*A high credit score is proof that
you are a good money manager.*

Conventional Wisdom

Credit Is Debt

You know that plastic thing you have in your wallet that says "Visa" or "MasterCard" on it? That thing that allows you to go to a store and instantly borrow money to purchase an item? What's it called? You would assume that a plastic card that allows you to incur debt would be called a *debt* card, but it isn't. It's called a *credit* card. Why is it not called a debt card? Because debt is a negative term, something to be avoided, whereas credit is good. It's a marketing strategy: the big banks know that you would be less likely to use a card that reminded you of the negative concept of debt every time you used it. Financial institutions know that we are guided by our emotions. Words matter, so they use words that trick our emotional minds into believing that the opposite is true, that debt is credit.

We've all heard the expression "give credit where credit is due." Credit in this sense is something you earn. It's positive. We like to give "credit for a job well done." Credit is considered to be a good thing, which is why it's called a credit card.

So would you use your credit card differently if it was called a debt card? Try it. Starting now, refer to your credit card only as a debt card. When you go to the store or gas station or wherever, say out loud, "I will complete this transaction by borrowing money on my debt card." Yes, the cashier will probably look at you funny, but even if you're a slow learner it will take only a dozen or two transactions before your mind will create a new association between your plastic card and debt.

The credit card companies have manipulated you into thinking that credit is good, and they do it constantly. Here's another example of how financial institutions manipulate us into thinking in a way that is opposite to our best interests: credit scores.

I Am a Good Person Because I Have a High Credit Score

Wrong—you are not necessarily a good person if you have a high credit score. You are a good person if you call your mother once a week and are kind to animals and little children. A high credit score is not in any way related to how good you are as a person.

Ask your friends. They will spout the conventional wisdom that having a high credit score proves that you are responsible with money because it means you pay your bills on time and you're not a reckless spender, racking up your credit cards in frequent orgies of spending. Your friends will agree that a high credit score proves you are a financial genius.

I disagree. Your credit score is simply a mathematical calculation developed for the benefit of institutions that want to lend you money. Your credit score is calculated using various factors including:

- Your payment history
- The amounts you owe
- The length of your credit history (longer is better)
- New credit you have recently obtained (to indicate that other lenders believe you are a good risk)
- Types of credit used

Your credit score is a measure of the risk to a lender, and of the probability that you will pay them back the money you borrow. A high credit score indicates that you are a low risk and, therefore, a lender will be willing to lend you more money. Let me emphasize this point again: a credit score is for the *benefit of the lender*, not for your benefit.

How do you get a high credit score? By proving to the credit-scoring agency that you are good at borrowing money and paying it back on time. Consider this example:

Sally is a self-made millionaire. She paid cash for her house and her car, and she hasn't borrowed money in twenty years. She has no credit cards, bank loans, or any other form of credit. She uses cash or her debit card for all purchases. Sally doesn't have a credit score, so it would be difficult for her to borrow money.

That's crazy, you say. Sally owns a house and a car. She has a good income. She could easily get a mortgage, so it's silly to say it would be difficult for her to borrow money. Not so fast, Sherlock. If Sally goes to a mortgage lender who cares only about the value of her house (an "asset-based" or "equity" lender), then yes, I agree, she would be able to get a mortgage. But if Sally goes to a traditional bank, the loan officer will grant a loan only if her credit score is above a pre-determined level. Because Sally has no credit score, a traditional bank may not be willing to give her a loan.

Consider now the case of Thomas:

> Thomas has five credit cards with a total credit limit of $50,000, against which he is currently carrying a total balance of $10,000. He always makes the minimum payments on his credit cards. As a result, Thomas has a very high credit score, so he would have no trouble qualifying for more debt at his bank.

Why does Thomas have a high credit score? One word: utilization. He has $50,000 in available limits on his credit cards and is carrying balances of "only" $10,000, so because his utilization is only 20 percent, he has a high credit score.

Let's ponder that for a minute: Thomas is borrowing $10,000 on credit cards at credit card interest rates and doesn't own a house or any other asset. According to his high credit score, he is a financial genius. But Sally, who has no debt and is paying nothing in interest, doesn't even have a credit score because she has no debt for the credit scoring agency to use to do the calculation. Who would you rather lend money to? The person with lots of assets and no debt, or the guy carrying balances on his credit cards?

In real life, the answer is easy. In the land of banker-make-believe, the guy with the credit card debt is "better." The banker loves the guy who doesn't pay off his balance in full each month but does make his minimum payments. That's the best of both worlds: he borrows just enough that the bank makes lots of money, but not so much that he can't continue to make the minimum payments. The bank doesn't want you to pay off debt immediately because there is no big profit in that. Similarly, the credit card company is thrilled if all you do is make your minimum payment each month, forever. They don't care if you never pay them back, as long as you stay in the "performing loan" category by making your minimum payments each month.

The Rule of 72

That can't be true, you say; the bank wants you to pay off your credit card eventually, don't they? No, they don't. They make more money if you pay forever. Let's look at an unrealistic but easy-to-understand example.

You get a loan from the bank and the bank says, "We will charge you interest at the rate of 18 percent per year, but you don't have to pay anything until you pay off the loan. We'll just add the interest to the loan." Cool.

So what will you owe in the future? You can calculate a precise answer with a calculator or a spreadsheet, but for a roughly correct answer that you can compute in your head, there is a quicker way: the Rule of 72. Take seventy-two and divide it by the interest rate, and you will get an approximation of the number of years it will take for the starting amount to double. So, according to the Rule of 72, it will take seventy-two divided by the interest rate of eighteen or approximately four years, for your loan balance to double.

Think of it this way: If you have a loan that carries an 18 percent interest rate, and all you do every month is pay just the interest, how much interest would you pay in four years? The answer is, the same amount as you originally borrowed. In other words, if all you do is make minimum payments each month in this scenario, you will end up paying back double the amount of the original loan—the principal you borrowed in the first place plus the interest, which has been compounding like mad while you've been deferring the inevitable.

Hard to believe? Let's take another simple example. Say you borrow $1,000 and make no payments. At 18 percent interest, you incur interest costs of $180 in the first year. After making no payments, at the end of the first year you owe a total of $1,180, and assuming you continue to make no payments, your total owing builds like this:

- Amount owing at start: $1,000
- $1,180 after Year 1

- $1,392.40 after Year 2
- $1,643.03 after Year 3
- $1,938.78 after Year 4

At the end of four years, you owe almost $2,000, or twice what you originally borrowed. If you now pay off the loan, the bank is thrilled. They doubled their money in four years. Beautiful. That's what the bank means when they refer to the "magic of compounding." The bank doesn't simply charge you interest on the amount you originally borrowed, it charges interest on the entire amount you owe: the amount outstanding on the original loan *and* all unpaid interest.

That's what compound interest is: interest on interest. Compound interest is great if you're an investor, but if you're a borrower, compound interest is a killer. If all you do is make whatever the bank defines as "minimum payments," and if those minimum payments don't include all of the interest you are being charged, your loan balance may be significantly increasing.

Of course, I am giving you a silly example. Banks don't give out loans where no payments are required for four years, so the interest you incur doesn't have the chance to compound over four years. Typically, with a line of credit or credit card you are required to pay the interest and a small amount of principal each month. But the concept is the same: the banks want you to make only the minimum payment because that's how they maximize the interest you pay.

The Credit Score Scam

If you want a high credit score, you need to have debt. Excessive debt is not good, and so, in many cases, a high credit score is not a worthwhile life goal. Obsessing over your credit score is not a good idea, but credit scores are important, right? If you want to get a loan at a low interest rate, you need a good credit score, and therefore conventional wisdom says that it's prudent to check your credit score before you apply for a loan. Conceptually, checking your credit score makes sense, but how do you do it?

You know the answer: the two big credit reporting agencies, Equifax and TransUnion, are very happy to sell you your credit score. You can pay a one-time fee and get your credit report that includes your credit score, instantly, online. Or you can sign up for their "monthly monitoring" service, whereby you pay a fee each month and get your credit score automatically every month. Selling your credit information to both the banks and to you is a very profitable business for the credit bureaus.

Here's the problem: your credit score may be meaningless. The credit score you buy from Equifax or TransUnion may not be the same credit score your lender is using to assess whether or not you get a loan, for two reasons. First, each credit-reporting agency may use their own formula for calculating your credit score, so they may each calculate a different score. Even if they use the same formula, each credit bureau may have different information, such as a different list of debts, and therefore they may calculate a different result. Second, your lender may get your credit score from Equifax, so if you only check your TransUnion score you won't know the credit score your lender is using to make their lending decision.

But wait, you say, "That makes no sense: I've heard of FICO scores, so they must all be the same." Wow, you are a perceptive reader. I'm glad you are not blindly believing everything I say. Well done. Let's dig deeper.

You are correct. FICO credit scores are a proprietary product, so every time a credit bureau uses a FICO score, they have to pay a fee to FICO (owned by the Fair Isaac Corporation, a huge company listed on the New York Stock Exchange). If you are running a credit bureau, here's a way to save money: don't use the FICO score, because you have to pay for it. Instead, make up your own score. Brilliant!

In early 2017 the Consumer Financial Protection Bureau in the United States ordered TransUnion and Equifax to pay $5.5 million in fines and give $17.6 million in refunds to consumers for falsely advertising credit scores for sale that they intimated were the same ones used by lenders, when in actual fact they weren't.[1] Both Equifax

---

1. *www.nbcnews.com/business/consumer/*
   free-credit-score-not-necessarily-credit-bureaus-busted-deception-n703146

and TransUnion denied violating any laws, but the message is clear: you don't know exactly what you are getting when you pay for your credit score.

In Canada, companies like Equifax use elements of the FICO score in their reporting. Lenders request your credit score directly from Equifax or TransUnion, so it may have elements of the FICO methodology in it, but there's a further twist: both credit bureaus have developed multiple scoring systems that they sell to lenders—not all of which you can see in your report.[1] One such score is produced by Equifax and is called the Bankruptcy Navigator Index, and it is used to predict the likelihood of a consumer filing bankruptcy in the next two years.[2] Checking your credit score alone does not alert you to the possibility that your lender may be using other scores to evaluate your loan.

So, should you pay to see your credit score? That's up to you. You may get the exact score the bank will use to evaluate your loan application, or you may get a score that's close to what the bank uses, or it may not be close at all. There is no guarantee that what you pay for is the same score that your potential lender will be using, so buyer beware.

But What About Free Credit Scores?

You may decide not to pay for a credit score because you don't want to waste money obtaining a score that may not be accurate or may not tell the whole story. But what about those services that offer you a free credit score? Even if the score is not completely accurate, if it's free, what's the harm?

Simple answer: nothing in life is free. I interviewed Kerry K. Taylor of Squawkfox.com[3] on my *Debt Free in 30* podcast,[4] and she told me that certain online lenders that offer a free credit score: ". . . have

1. *www.fico.com/en/newsroom/equifax-canada-and-fico-introduce-beacon-90-credit-score-07-03-2012*
2. *www.equifax.com/business/bankruptcy-navigator-index*
3. *www.squawkfox.com/*
4. *www.hoyes.com/blog/mogo-loans-are-they-a-good-deal/*

all of these data-crunching algorithms on the back end that look at the kind of prospective client that you're going to be as a borrower. They use data crunching, they use online tools, in order to get customers to apply for loans."

What Kerry's referring to is what happens when you go to a website that offers a free credit score and you enter your personal information, giving them permission to access your credit report. Sounds innocuous enough, right? Nope. By granting access to your credit report, you have now given that company complete access to a massive amount of your personal information. They now know where you live, where you work, and your complete debt history. They can now use this information to pitch you a loan.

Here's how it works: You fill out the "give me my free credit score" form, and instantly the computer analyzes your details and offers you a loan that meets the *lender's* risk profile. They may offer you a $1,000 high-interest, short-term loan (if your credit is bad), or a $5,000 regular-term loan at a still-high interest rate (if your credit is better). You just wanted a free credit score, but now that a loan is being dangled in front of you, the temptation to resist may be too great and you may click on the "sure, give me a loan" button, in which case your free credit score will now cost you a lot of interest—on a loan that you probably didn't need.

Remember: Nothing is free, even a free credit score. *Caveat emptor.*

Worrying About Your Credit Score Is Missing the Point

Conventional wisdom says you should do whatever you can to improve your credit score. A high credit score will make it easier for you to borrow more money, and at a lower interest rate. If your goal is to be the person who can borrow the most money at the lowest interest rate, great, go for it; but if your goal is to be financially prudent, excessive borrowing should not be your goal.

You have a choice. You can be like Sally and have lots of assets, no debt, and no credit score; or you can be like Thomas, who has debt that he pays a high interest rate on each month and, therefore, has a high credit score.

You are not a financial genius because you have a high credit score. You are financially responsible if you have no debt, or as little debt as possible. Having no debt won't improve your credit score, but it is the most basic element of financial security.

Saving money and investing are critical to a sound financial future, but *saving money is not a section on your credit report.* Your credit report deals only with debt. (See how this chapter ties together brilliantly? I know what you're thinking: "It should be called a *debt* report!" Exactly! Well done.)

Practical Advice: Focus on Your Goals, Not Your Credit Score

Don't obsess over your credit score, because if you do, you are more likely to spend money on credit-score reporting services that may not even be giving you the actual score the bank will be using to evaluate your loan application. Obsessing over your credit score may also cause you to take out more loans than you need, which may eventually work against your attempt to increase your credit score.

If you are planning to apply for a big car loan or mortgage and you want to evaluate your chances of getting a loan, you can pay for your credit score if you wish; it's not that much money if you do it only sporadically. You now know that the credit score you buy may not be exactly what the bank will see, but if it gives you an approximate indication of your credit status, there is probably no harm in obtaining it.

My advice would be to get a copy of your credit report directly from Equifax and TransUnion, both of which are required to give you a report for free once a year so that you can confirm that there are no obvious errors on it. The free credit report does not include your credit score, but if all of the information is correct, the credit score is of little relevance.

I would then focus on the basics:

- Be prudent with your spending.
- Work to improve your income.
- Save money.
- Don't borrow excessively.

These strategies may not help your credit score; they may even make it lower, but that's fine, because these basic strategies will improve your cash flow and reduce your debt, which is in your best interests. After all, your goal is to improve your financial position. Your goal is not to make the banks rich by focusing on a credit score that was developed entirely for their benefit, not yours. You are the boss.

[Myth #5]

THE MOST IMPORTANT NUMBER IS THE MONTHLY PAYMENT

The car salesman says you can drive the car off the lot for a small payment of only $189 bi-weekly. You can easily afford the $189, so nothing else matters. It's a no-brainer: buy the car.

Conventional Wisdom

The Monthly Payment Is Almost Irrelevant

The notion that "only the monthly payment matters" is ridiculous, and of all of the myths I will discuss in this book, this is the easiest one to dispel. It's like shooting ducks in a barrel, as the old saying goes. So, let's shoot some ducks, starting with the real story of John.

John wants to buy a new car. He wants the car to have turbo because John is a guy, and guys want to buy cars that say "turbo" on the back. John doesn't know what "turbo" means, but it sounds fast, so he wants it. John, like all guys and gals, is ruled by his emotions.

The finance guy at the dealership gives John two options: he can pay $718 per month and have the car paid off sooner, or he can opt for a cheaper monthly payment of $511 and take longer to own the car outright. John is most concerned about his monthly cash flow, so he picks the $511 deal because it's cheaper.

But John has made a silly decision because he didn't review the math. Here's the story the numbers tell: The car costs $30,000. If John makes no down payment and, if we ignore taxes and other costs, he makes forty-eight monthly payments at a 7 percent interest rate, his payments are $718.39 per month. In total, over four years he will pay $34,482.72. If John stretches the loan over seventy-two months (six years), the monthly payment drops to $511.47, in which case, over six years he will pay a total of $36,825.84. In other words, extending a loan for two additional years lowers the monthly payment but increases the total amount paid, in John's case by over $2,300.

The monthly payment is only one factor in the total cost of the loan and we can tweak this example by changing the other terms of the loan, but you get the idea. Some of the other factors to consider when getting a car loan include:

- Interest rate
- Down payment
- Amortization period (the length of the loan)
- Residual value (more common in leases, it's the guaranteed value at the end of the term)
- Mileage limits (again more common in leases; if you go over the mileage limit you pay significant extra charges at the end of the term)

You can search the Internet for many different online loan calculators that allow you to play with the numbers to determine the impact each change will make to the total cost of the loan, but here's one more basic example: A down payment of $2,000 reduces the $30,000 loan to $28,000. Using the same interest rate as in the previous example, over a four-year loan the savings are $2,299.20, and over six years the savings are $2,455.20.

In summary, the monthly payment is only one aspect of the cost of a car, or any other loan. And simply focusing on making this monthly number the lowest it can be is not usually the smartest financial decision in the long run.

Isn't This Obvious?

You are an attentive reader, so after reading the previous section you said to yourself, "That was obvious." Obviously making payments for six years will cost more than making payments for four years. Obviously a larger down payment will reduce the total cost. Yes, when you think about it, it is obvious. But the problem, in my experience, is that we don't think about it. We *want* to buy that car, so we don't take the time to consider all of the facts carefully.

Redundant News Flash: We think that as humans we are rational, but we are irrational beings. We think we bought the car we are currently driving because it has the best gas mileage or the highest safety rating or a high ranking on some other tangible, quantifiable scale. But nope.

The truth is, you selected the car you're driving car because it's the make you always buy, or it's the first one the salesman showed you, or you liked where the cup holders are, or some other not-exactly-rational reason. Then, once you picked out the car, you looked for rational reasons to justify your gut instinct.

When you go to a car dealership, who do you talk to first: the car salesman or the finance guy? The answer, of course, is the car salesman, because they want to sell you the car. There's no point in discussing financing until you know how much you are financing. It's the same when you want to buy a house. You find the house you want to buy, and then you talk to the bank about a mortgage. But this is backwards. Unless you are paying cash, the financing analysis should be the first step, not the last, *if you are making a rational decision.*

I have met hundreds of people over the years, mostly males, who are seriously stretched financially and yet are paying half of their monthly income for their car. If I ask them, "How much does your car cost?" they will tell me, "$500 per month," but of course that's just the monthly loan payment. When they add in gas, insurance, and repairs and maintenance, it's not unusual for the total expense to equal half of their income. How is that possible? They didn't crunch the numbers before buying the car. They started with the car, and then crunched the numbers.

This is also a common problem with people who get debt consolidation loans. They have three credit cards at 19 percent interest and their minimum payments each month total $800. They go to a finance company and get a consolidation loan, and now they have only one monthly payment of just $600. Great!

Not so great, actually, because the monthly payment doesn't matter. What matters is the total they will pay over the life of the loan. The debt consolidation loan has an interest rate of 33 percent and will last for eight years, so it would have been much cheaper simply to keep paying the credit cards. If you focus only on the monthly payment and ignore the interest rate and amortization period, it's easy to make this mistake.

Practical Advice: Crunch the Numbers

The monthly payment is only one factor to consider when analyzing a loan. You must also consider other factors like the interest rate, the term of the loan, and the total amount you will pay on the loan in order to make an informed decision. If you look at all of the facts, you may decide that that loan isn't worth it after all.

You are not a rational being. None of us is. We follow our gut instinct. Sometimes this is a great strategy. (If you are being chased by a lion, don't think, run.) But in most cases, we could all benefit from some rational thought and analysis. To overcome your built-in bias to follow your gut, crunch the numbers first, and then let your gut take over. That's a win-win.

[Myth #6]

BANK AT ONLY ONE BANK

You get the best deal if you do all of your banking with one bank, so be sure to have your mortgage, credit cards, car loan, insurance, and all investments with one bank.

Conventional Wisdom

There Are Two Problems with Having Just One Bank

Your bank will tell you it's a question of convenience. Do you want to be racing around from bank to bank to do your business, or would you prefer a "one-stop shop"? On the surface, dealing with just one bank makes sense, because who wants to run around from bank to bank? (Of course, you hardly ever actually set foot inside a bank. They have eliminated most tellers and you can do almost everything electronically now, but you'll never hear that side of the discussion from a bank.)

I understand. It's nice to be able to log in to your bank's website portal and see information about your bank account, credit card, line of credit, and mortgage. It's nice that your car insurance is from the same bank and you can easily pay it with a pre-authorized payment. It's simple. Convenient. But there is a dark side to having all of your eggs in one banking basket. Two dark sides, actually.

Dark Side #1: Fees

This is a relatively minor issue, but it's worth considering: bank fees. You switch to a new bank, and they offer you a great deal. Today only, for new customers, they have a deal: if you maintain a minimum balance of $1,000 in your new account, you'll get free deposits, free electronic transfers, and even a free toaster. Great. Unfortunately though, this is a limited-time offer. At some point in the future, the sweet deal becomes not so sweet. You will then need a minimum of a $5,000 balance to get all of the free stuff (minus the toaster), and your service charges gradually increase.

So why don't the banks worry that when they start increasing their fees you'll just switch to another bank, with a better deal? Because that's not how we humans work. We are not rational (yes, this is a common theme in this book). We take the path of least resistance, and switching banks is a hassle. Your pay is directly deposited by your employer, so now you have to go to Edna in payroll and give her your new banking information and hope that she processes it correctly. Then you have to contact all of your pre-authorized payments (hydro, telephone, cable TV, etc.) and switch them to your new account. One of them doesn't get switched in time, so when they try to take it from your old bank account, there's no money there and you get hit with an NSF charge, and any money you saved in fees by taking advantage of the new-customer deal are now irrelevant.

But that's not all: Every bank now assumes you are engaged in some elaborate money-laundering scheme. Gone are the days when you could just walk into a bank and open a new account. Now you need three forms of identification, including photo ID, plus a letter of reference from your employer and a credit check, and hey, how about a blood and urine sample while you're at it?

Because of this, switching bank accounts is a hassle, so the banks know that once you are with them, you are with them for life. Here's a telling question: How many different banks have you dealt with in your life?

In my case, I opened my first bank account as a child, and it was where my parents banked. When I got married we opened a joint account at my wife's bank because, being the smart one in the family, she had a better deal at her bank than I had at mine. So, in over half a century on this planet, my primary banking relationship has been with a grand total of two banks. Two. I'm guessing your number is similar.

The banks understand inertia. They know you are unlikely to switch banks, so they have no incentive to give you a better deal once you are already a customer. By having more than one bank account, you can more easily compare deals and switch your banking to the best deal at that time.

The creep of ever-increasing fees is a problem when you deal with only one bank, but that's not the most significant issue, as we will discuss next.

Dark Side #2: You Lose Control

If you bank at one bank, you are at their mercy. Just ask Rob.

> Rob is self-employed. Due to an error made by his accountant, his taxes didn't get paid on time and the government froze his bank account. He had no access to cash and no bank account to use to deposit money from his clients.

I have greatly simplified Rob's story, but it's a story I've heard many times. The details are not important. If you have only one bank account, at one bank, and that bank account becomes frozen, you have no access to money. In Rob's case, what's worse is that he now doesn't have a bank account into which he can deposit money from his customers, so he can't deposit the funds he needs to use to pay his mortgage and car loan and to buy supplies for his business. He's got a problem.

What's the solution? First, hire a better accountant, and make sure your taxes are paid on time. Second, stop blaming your accountant. If you want to be self-employed, it is your responsibility to understand your obligations, including tax payments, and get them paid on time. Third, have a second bank account, at a different bank. That second bank account should be an account at a bank where you don't owe any money, and it should be an "active" account, meaning you have at least a few dollars in it and you occasionally make a deposit to keep it active.

If Rob had a second bank account that he never used to pay the government, it's unlikely they would have frozen it, so Rob could have used it to deposit payments from his customers and pay his bills.

You may not be self-employed, and you don't owe the government any money, so there's no need to have a second bank account, right? Wrong. Check out Fred's story:

Fred was smart and set up six months' worth of automatic payments from his bank account at XYZ Bank to his credit card at XYZ Bank. But, at the end of the six months, Fred forgot to set up a new series of automatic payments, and he missed paying his credit card bill for two months. So XYZ Bank went into his bank account and scooped the money for the missing payments, plus extra interest and service charges. This left Fred short, unbeknownst to him, so his mortgage and car payment bounced, which led to another group of service charges and extra fees.

This situation was Fred's fault; he didn't make his payments, and the fine print on his credit card agreement essentially says, "If you don't make your payments, we can go into your bank account and scoop the money." Of course, though, the fine print is small consolation for Fred. So what's the solution?

Separate your liabilities from your assets. Have your debt at one bank and your assets at another. If you have a credit card and a bank account at XYZ Bank, it's easy for them to go into your account and take their money. It's the same bank, so there's no need for a court order or any special power to get your money. Therefore, if you have a credit card at XYZ Bank, have your pay deposited into ABC Bank. That way, if there's a problem, it's not as easy for XYZ Bank to take their money automatically.

But wait, you say, I pay my bills on time, so there is no need to have a separate bank account, correct? Nope. Look at what happened to Tom:

> Tom banks at ABC Bank. There was a massive computer outage at ABC Bank, and his debit card and credit card didn't work for two days. He couldn't get cash or even fill up his car with gas.

Impossible, you say? I can tell you that it most certainly is possible, because it happened to me. Technology isn't perfect, and so it's possible for a credit card company or bank to have a computer problem. But if you have a second credit card or a second debit card from a second bank, a problem at your main bank won't prevent you from having access to emergency funds.

Practical Advice: Spread Your Wealth

You are the boss and, as such, you should do what is right for you, not what is best for the bank. Your bank will make it sound really easy and convenient for you to bank with them and only them, but that kind of exclusivity is much better for them than it is for you.

Sure, there are benefits to dealing with only one bank, such as a better deal on service charges, but are the benefits enough to make it worth it? Most people don't think about the downsides. To manage your risk and safeguard your money as much as possible, it's a good idea to spread your wealth around a bit. Consider having one main bank that you deal with for most things. That's where your pay is deposited, where you have a credit card, and that's the account you use to pay all of your bills. Because you do a lot of business with that bank, you will likely get a good deal on service charges and enjoy good service (when you go into the branch and they see what you have on deposit, they will treat you well).

But also make sure you deal with a secondary bank where you have a few dollars on deposit. If, for example, you have an emergency need for cash and the debit machine is not working at your main bank, you are not completely out of luck.

You might even take this one step further and have a second credit card as well, one that is not from your main bank. My wife and I have a joint bank account, but she also has another credit card, not with our bank, that is entirely in her name; so again, if there is a problem with our bank, or with our account, she's got a second option.

How many bank accounts and credit cards is enough? How many is too many? That's up to you. Personally, I think two of each is a good number. Any more than that and it's too much to keep track of, and you risk paying too much in service charges. However, that decision is up to you.

My point is this: Don't allow all of your finances to be tied up in one financial institution so that you are in a situation where they are in more control of your money than you are. You are the boss, not the bank.

[Myth #7]

WHEN A COLLECTION AGENT CALLS, ALWAYS PAY UP

Collection agents don't fool around. If you don't pay what you owe, they will take you to court, sue you, garnishee your wages, and ruin your credit forever. If they call, pay them.

Conventional Wisdom

What You Don't Know about Collection Agents

When your money problems go from bad to worse—you're stretched too thin, you can't pay your bills, and your debts are mounting—you often end up being put into collections by one or more of your creditors. Banks and credit card companies don't want to do the "dirty work" of collecting, so they hire a collection agency to collect the money they are owed.

If you have ever been on the receiving end of calls from a collection agency, you know they are persistent, worrisome, and sometimes very threatening. It's stressful, and you feel that you have no choice but to pay up. But do you have to pay them? What happens if you ignore a collection agency's threats? Let's review the collection process to understand how it works and to better understand the true powers of the collection agent.

Every collection story I hear follows a standard sequence of events:

1. Everything is going great. You're paying all of your bills on time.

2. Something happens (e.g., job loss, medical issue, divorce) and you're unable to make the minimum payment on your credit card that month. Because you have always paid your bills on time, at the end of the month your credit card statement has a friendly note that says, "We have not received your payment this month. Please make your payment. If you have already made your payment, please disregard this notice."

3. You can't make your payment the next month either, so now the phone calls start. The first phone call from the bank credit card representative is friendly, just giving you a "heads up" that your payment wasn't received and asking, "Is there anything we can do to help?" The note on your credit card statement this month is somewhat harsher, intimating: "This is serious: make your payment or bad things will happen."

4. By month number three, the friendly approach is over. The bank collector calls to tell you they have suspended your card and payment in full is due immediately. No more Mister Nice Guy. You protest and say you have been a perfect customer for

twenty years and this is "just a little rough patch, can't you give me more time?" Nope. They are turning your account over to a third-party collection agency.

5. At some point in month four, or five, or six, you receive a letter from a third-party collection agency. The letter says that they have taken over collection activities for the bank. You may no longer discuss this with the bank. All payments must now be made to the third-party collection agency. They call you daily and send you letters weekly, for about two months.

6. After two months of intense third-party collection activity, assuming you are still unable to pay, they go silent. The daily calls stop. The letters stop. You hear nothing, for about a month.

7. Then you get a letter and a phone call from a different collection agency. The cycle begins again.

This is how banks and credit card companies collect past-due amounts. For the first ninety days or so, an internal bank employee does the collecting. At that point, you are still considered a customer of the bank, and the representative wants to do what they can to salvage the relationship and return you to the status of a profitable customer. They are friendly and try to work with you. If you can make a partial payment, they will keep working with you. If you still have decent credit, they may give you a line of credit or a loan to pay off your credit card so that they can move you from the "in arrears" category to the "performing loans" category.

The exact time limit is different for each bank, but after somewhere between 90 and 120 days of no payments, the bank decides that you are no longer salvageable. The relationship is over. You are no longer welcome as a customer. Bye-bye. They don't care that you were a great customer for twenty years. They don't care that they have made thousands of dollars in profit from you. Once they decide that your debt is uncollectible, it's over. And that's when they send your account to a third-party collection agency.

"Third party" means it is no longer the bank that will call you. You will now get letters and calls from "ABC Collection Company" or some such name. (Very often the collection agency has a name that is just a series of letters, meaningless, signifying nothing.) Why doesn't the bank just keep collecting? Why send you somewhere else? Two reasons.

First, bank employees are expensive. They work in a nice office building, the bank pays them a decent salary and benefits, and the bank contributes to a pension for them. This amounts to a significant cost, so if the bank doesn't think it can recover that cost, it won't spend the money collecting from you. A collection agency will generally have employees who are paid less than bank employees, and they likely don't have benefits or a pension. The bank saves a lot of money by outsourcing collection activities to a third-party collection agency.

(Incidentally, over the years I have done bankruptcies for dozens of collection-agency employees. Most of them at one time had a better-paying job, but when they lost that job they started working at a collection agency because they had to find work. Collection jobs are not high-paying, and many of those jobs are not full time. I know of many collectors who get only three hours of work a day, between 4:00 p.m. and 7:00 p.m., because that's when people tend to be home. The collection agency doesn't want to pay for employees to call when no one is home, so they save a lot of money by having only part-time employees.)

Second, the bank doesn't want to "look bad." The bank wants to present their employees as helpful and friendly. Having employees calling to collect money doesn't help the bank's image or reputation.

When the bank outsources collection activities, the third-party collection agency is doing the "dirty work," so any bad feelings you may have about the process are directed toward the collection agency, not the bank.

Why do you get a phone call from one collection agency for the first few months and then start getting calls from a different one? Different agencies handle different stages of collection. The first agency that calls you (what they call the "first hand-off") is dealing with you as a relatively current customer. The debt is only a few months old, so there is a reasonably good chance that they will be able to collect at least a portion of the amount owing. This agency earns a relatively modest commission, perhaps 20 percent of the amount collected. If you owe $1,000, the collection agency may offer to settle with you for $800 if you can pay that as a lump sum. The agency earns a 20 percent commission ($160), the bank gets the rest ($640), and everyone is happy.

However, if the first agency has no success collecting, they'll return your file to the bank and the bank will then send it to a different agency (the second hand-off). That's why there is often a lull in collection activity. The phone calls stop for a period of time while your file is in between agencies. The second agency is now dealing with an older file, and their chances of collecting are reduced, so this agency probably earns a larger commission, uses more aggressive tactics, and likely has greater latitude in proposing a settlement. For example, they may earn a 40 percent commission, and they may be willing to settle for only $600 on the original $1,000 debt.

As I said at the start of this book, you should question everything I write, and this chapter is no exception. I don't work for a collection agency and I am not privy to the contracts the banks sign with their collection agents, so I don't know exactly what each agency earns. Each deal is different, but the basic principles are the same with each agency.

Collection Agencies Earn a Commission

A common misconception is that the collection agency that is collecting the money gets to keep it because they own your debt. For debts under a year old, that is almost never the case. Banks will sell very old debts, but they very rarely sell relatively new debts because it is not profitable to do so.

It is very common for banks and credit card companies to sell the debts of debtors who are already bankrupt or in a consumer proposal (which is a legal process, under federal law, administered by a Licensed Insolvency Trustee, whereby a debtor makes a deal with his or her creditors to pay less than the full amount owing). The bank can estimate, based on past history, what they are likely to generate in an insolvency filing. They may get two or three cents on the dollar in a bankruptcy (in most bankruptcies they get nothing, but they get more in some; so on average they get a few cents), and 30 cents or more in a consumer proposal. It may take up to five years for the bank to get the entire 30 cents in a consumer proposal, so they will often sell that client to a debt buyer, perhaps for 20 cents, and the debt buyer then collects the 30 cents over time.

An insolvency is a unique situation. In most cases, a bank will not sell a debt because the debt buyer is willing to pay only a few cents on the dollar. For such a low return, it's more profitable for the bank to hire a collection agency and generate higher returns. This is not to say that banks never sell old debts; they do, but they are generally very old debts where the bank has no reasonable expectation of collecting more than a penny or two on the dollar.

This is why it's difficult to make a great deal with a collection agency. If a debt buyer paid 5 cents on the dollar for your debt, they are happy to make a deal with you and collect 50 cents on the dollar. They make ten times their money. But if the collection agency does not own your debt and is earning a commission only on the amount they collect, they can't make much of a profit if they heavily discount the debt. If you owe $1,000 and they settle for $500, but they get only a 20 percent commission, the collection agency earns only $100, so they are less inclined to give you a big discount on your debt.

Now that we've discussed how collection agencies work, let's get to the point of this chapter: why you should never pay a collection agency. Here's Dennis's story:

> Dennis was doing well but then got injured at work and was unable to pay his credit card. The bank called him for three months before handing him off to a collection agency, and then a second collection agency. They told him they would sue him and garnishee his wages and ruin his credit if he didn't pay them.

So what should Dennis do? Pay them? If Dennis has the money then yes, he should pay them, but obviously, if Dennis had the money we wouldn't be having this discussion. If he had the money he would have paid the bank and the debt would never have gone to a collection agency in the first place.

Here's the big secret that collection agents will never tell you: **collection agencies almost never sue anyone**. It's true. Why? Because it costs money to sue someone. To start a lawsuit, even in small claims court, it requires many steps. While it is possible to start a lawsuit without a lawyer, it's common practice to use a law firm for legal matters. The lawyer must create a statement of claim and serve it on the debtor, often by using either registered mail or a process server, so that they have proof of service when they get to court. They must pay a court fee to start the lawsuit, and the lawyer must appear in court on the hearing date. That adds up to a lot of expense. If the debtor has no money and can't pay the claim, that's a lot of money spent for no return. But the cost of a lawsuit is not the main reason that collection agencies rarely sue anyone.

As we know, collection agencies earn a commission on what they collect, and that makes lawsuits impractical. If it's a $1,000 debt and the collection agency's commission is $200, the most they can earn is $200. If it costs $300 to pay the lawyer, the process server, and the court costs, the collection agency loses money even if they win! The math doesn't work.

It is standard practice in a lawsuit to ask the court for an award of costs, so if I incur $300 in costs to sue you and I win, I will ask the court to award an extra $300, so that then I have a judgment for $1,300. If I'm the collection agency I would get my $200 commission plus get my $300 in costs, so it makes sense to sue, right? Wrong. It's too risky. There is no guarantee that the agency will win the lawsuit, and even if they do, there is no guarantee that the judge will award costs. But this isn't the greatest risk. The greatest risk is that the debtor doesn't have the money to pay.

In a typical lawsuit to collect a credit card debt, the objective is to get a judgment, and then enforce that judgment by garnisheeing wages, or seizing assets. Why did the debtor not pay their debt? It may be that they don't have a job, and therefore don't have the income to make payments. Getting a garnishment order against someone who doesn't have a job is pointless. If a debtor has assets, they could have sold them or refinanced them and paid off their debt. They didn't pay off their debt, so it's likely they don't have any assets; again, getting a judgment against nothing is pointless. This is why collection agencies almost never sue anyone. It costs money, and time, and it's likely they won't collect enough to cover their costs, so there is no point in suing anyone.

Do banks sue? Yes, banks and credit card companies and other lenders will sue debtors who don't pay. If you bank with ABC Bank and have a credit card with ABC Bank and you don't pay your credit card bill, ABC Bank has a decision to make: sue, or not? If you bank with them, they see your pay being deposited every week into your bank account, so they know you have a job and they know how much you make, so it's a much less-risky decision for the bank to start legal action. They can reasonably predict success, so suing makes sense.

If you have a mortgage with ABC Bank, ABC Bank knows where you live and they can easily determine what your house is worth as well as what's owing on it. If they see that it has equity, it makes sense to attempt to get a judgment, because they could, theoretically, force the sale of your house to collect their money. The odds are in their favor.

To summarize: banks sue, credit card companies sue, but collection agencies typically don't sue.

How the Statute of Limitations Works against Collection Agencies

But wait! There's more! Collection agencies only collect old debts. The bank waits at least three months, and often much longer, before turning an account over to a third-party collection agency. The second hand-off may not happen for at least a year or more, which is why we know that collection agencies are dealing with older debts.

In most provinces and states there are Limitations Acts, legislation that prescribes the time periods under which a lawsuit must be commenced. For example, in Ontario, Canada, the *Limitations Act* specifies that, for a standard business debt like a credit card or bank loan, the lender must commence their legal action within two years of the last activity date, which is typically the last payment made by the debtor.

Every jurisdiction has different laws, and I'm not a lawyer, so don't blindly believe the specifics of what I'm saying, but be aware of the general concept: In most cases, a bank can't wait forever before suing you. The courts don't want to hear lawsuits based on events from ten years ago. The original documents aren't available, witnesses may not be available, and so governments have decided that time limits are necessary. Makes sense.

That's yet another reason why a collection agency likely won't sue you. If they did, and you understand the limitation periods in your jurisdiction, by the time you appeared in court, you could tell the judge the debt is too old and the case would be thrown out. That's wasted time and money for the collection agency.

Why Do Collection Agents Want a Small Payment?

Why will collection agents often ask for a "good faith" payment? "Hey, Joe," they might say. "I want to help. If you could just send us $10 to keep your account active, I can convince my boss not to take you to court." Sounds reasonable, but if Joe sends the $10, he has made a big mistake. Why? Because the collection agent wasn't going to sue him anyway, for all the reasons we've just looked at. But now that Joe has paid even a small amount, there is new activity on the account, and the limitation period has restarted.

If the limitation period in this jurisdiction is two years, and if Joe hasn't made a payment for twenty months, there are only four months to go before the creditor loses the ability to take legal action. However, if Joe makes a $10 payment, the clock resets and now the creditor has twenty-four months to commence legal action. This is why it almost never makes sense to pay a collection agency.

Let me repeat the key points:

- Collection agents almost never sue anyone (although they threaten it all the time).
- Creditors generally have time restrictions governing when they can commence legal action; by not paying, you reduce the chance that they will ever legally be able to launch a successful lawsuit.

Practical Advice: How to Deal with Collection Agents

Here's my advice: if you owe money to the original lender, like your bank or credit card company, work out a plan with them directly to pay them back. They can and may sue you, and non-payment will certainly negatively impact your credit score (not to mention, calls from collection agencies are a hassle); so if you can pay, pay.

If, however, your account has been turned over to a third-party collection agency, it pays for you to know your rights. In many jurisdictions, these companies are required to notify you in writing before making a collection call. Ask for proof that you owe the money. If you have the money to pay, either in full or at a discount, propose a settlement and, if they agree, ask them to send you a release letter before you send the collection agency any money. A release letter simply says, "ABC Bank agrees to accept $XXX in full and final settlement of the debt owed by Joe Smith re: account #123." Having this release letter offers you some protection in the event the collection agency later claims that you have not fully paid the debt.

If you don't have the money to pay or if you can't reach a suitable settlement with the collection agency, **don't pay them anything**. Partial payments don't make the phone calls stop. In fact, a partial payment does the opposite: it proves to the bill collector that you have money, so they will increase their collection efforts. Worse yet, even a small payment restarts the clock on the limitation period, which preserves the collection agency's or the original creditor's right to sue you in the future. A small payment helps them but hurts you.

Ultimately, if you have more debt than you can handle and you can't work out a settlement, a bankruptcy may be necessary, but paying a collection agent is almost never a good option.

[Myth #8]

PAY YOUR SMALL DEBTS FIRST

If you are in debt, pay off your small debts first. It will give you a feeling of accomplishment, and keep you motivated to pay off your larger debts.

Conventional Wisdom

Math or Psychology?

From a math point of view, this myth is easy. Follow the money. From a psychology point of view, not so much.

Let's assume you have two debts:

- $5,000 store credit card at 29 percent interest
- $500 bank credit card at 9 percent interest

The proper strategy appears obvious: pay off the high-interest debt first, because this strategy will spare you the most in interest. Of course, you should make your minimum payments on both cards so you don't get charged additional fees, but any extra money you have should go toward paying down the 29 percent–interest credit card, because obviously that will save you 29 percent interest. Makes sense.

Conventional wisdom, however, takes a more holistic, psychological view of your debt issues, believing that you will feel better about yourself if you can clean up your small debts first. By paying off your $500 credit card, regardless of the interest rate, you will shorten your list of debts, which will reduce your stress and allow you to focus on the bigger debts. While this strategy makes no sense mathematically, I understand the thought process. As irrational, emotional beings, we feel better succeeding in paying off the small debt first.

To take an extreme example, let's assume you have ten small debts of $200 each and one large debt of $10,000. Each of the $200 debts has a different payment due date, so you spend time every month juggling your payments to make sure that everything gets paid on time. By paying off your small debts first, you will simplify your life and make budgeting easier. I totally get it.

But let's not forget about the math. It may be a nuisance to juggle all of your payments, but it's costing you actual money to be paying high interest on your larger debt. This leaves you with a decision to make: pay more in interest and stay in debt longer, or deal with the nuisance factor of having many small debts.

A Repayment Strategy

If you have small and large debts with varying interest rates, start by making a list of all of the debts, including the amount owing and the interest rate. I would then prioritize them as follows:

- The highest priority would be the debts with the highest interest rate.
- The second-highest priority would be callable or secured debts.

Simple.

Before we discuss callable or secured debts, a final word on small debts: I do understand the nuisance factor of having several of them; so if you have very small debts with lower interest rates that can be paid off in a month or two, fine, go for it. Pay them off. It's actually costing you more in interest if you pay them as opposed to using that money to pay down your higher interest rate debt, but if the amounts owing are small, the interest savings are not that significant. And the positive karma from simplifying your financial life is probably worth it. You are the boss. You decide.

Callable and Secured Debts

A *callable* debt is exactly what the name implies: the lender can "call" the debt, or demand payment, at any time. A line of credit may be an example of a callable debt. It's an open line of credit, with no fixed terms of repayment. If the bank decides to increase the interest rate tomorrow, it can. If it decides to reduce your credit limit tomorrow, it can. If you have a $20,000 line of credit and you are borrowing the full $20,000, and the bank decides to reduce your authorized credit limit to zero, they just "called" your loan.

An example of an "un-callable" loan (which is a name I just made up) would be a mortgage, car loan, or any other loan with fixed terms of repayment. If I have a car loan from the bank that requires me to pay $400 per month for thirty more months, the bank can't call my loan, provided I'm honoring the terms of the loan (that is, paying the $400 each month). Similarly, as long as I make my mortgage payments as agreed, I keep my house. A mortgage is not a callable loan.

Consider this situation:

Sally has a fixed-term loan for $10,000 and an unsecured line of credit for $10,000. They both have the same interest rate. Which debt should she pay off first?

Because both loans are the same amount, there is no "size" priority, and because both loans charge the same rate of interest, there is no interest-rate advantage to paying one off as opposed to the other. This means the decision comes down to the status of the loan. If I were Sally, I would pay down the callable loan (her line of credit) first. I would pay it down first because I understand that the bank could "call" it at any time.

Why would the bank call your loan? Many reasons. A vice president at a large Canadian bank once told me that his bank does a credit check on all of their borrowing customers every three months. It's a "soft hit," which doesn't appear as an inquiry on your credit report, so it doesn't hurt your credit score. The bank does it as an early warning system. If the bank notices that you have taken on a lot of new debt, it may decide that you are becoming a riskier customer, which may lead it to increase your interest rate or reduce the amount you can borrow.

What would happen if your $10,000 line of credit at 7 percent interest instantly became a $5,000 line of credit at 15 percent interest? With a callable loan, the bank can change the terms at any time, with minimal notice to you. If you were planning on borrowing against your line of credit next month and the bank suddenly chops your limit in half, what are you going to do? Replace it with higher interest rate debt? This is why paying off callable debt first is a prudent strategy. You put control of your debt back into your hands, making you the boss.

A *secured* debt is a debt that is attached to, or secured by, an asset, and one that is also worthy of consideration for early payment. Common examples of secured debt would be a car loan (secured by a car) or a mortgage (secured by a house).

The advantage of a secured loan to you, the borrower, is that a secured loan generally charges the lowest possible interest rate, because secured loans are the least-risky type of loan for the bank. If you don't pay your mortgage, the bank will take your house and sell it to recover the loan. In most cases the bank recovers all of their money, so because there is very little risk to the bank, it can charge a low interest rate.

This is why it's unlikely that a secured loan would carry the same interest rate as an unsecured loan. When you are prioritizing your loan repayments, you are highly unlikely to find that your secured debt carries the highest interest rate. For example, in almost all cases, a credit card will have a much higher interest rate than a mortgage, so the repayment decision is simple.

But what do you do if you have an unsecured debt and a secured debt with the same interest rate? Consider paying off the secured debt first. Have a look at what happened to Amanda:

Amanda has a $10,000 unsecured debt consolidation loan and a $10,000 car loan. They are both fixed-term loans, with the same interest rate and the same monthly payment. Both loans have a prepayment privilege by which Amanda can make a "double up" payment any month, with no penalties. Amanda gets a tax refund and a bonus at work, and she uses that extra money to repay her debt consolidation loan. Then Amanda loses her job and falls behind on her car-loan payments. The bank won't give her another loan because she doesn't have a job, and so eventually they repossess her car.

Bummer. In Amanda's case, she should have paid off her car loan first and then started making extra payments on her debt consolidation loan. Once the car loan is paid off, the lender can't repossess the car, so paying it off first is good protection for Amanda.

Let me point out that again I am giving you an unrealistic example. It's unlikely that an unsecured debt consolidation loan would carry the same terms, conditions, and interest rate as a secured car loan (although it is possible, particularly if you get a consolidation loan at a teaser rate at the bank).

Practical Advice: Set Your Priorities

To summarize: If it makes you feel better to eliminate debt by paying off small loans first, fine; just be aware that you will pay more interest in the long run by paying off small, lower interest rate debts before higher interest rate debts. You must look deep within your soul and determine if you are a "get it off my list" person or an "I want to save money" person. There is an obviously correct mathematical answer; only you can answer the psychological question. Fortunately, now that you are conscious of the fact that we are irrational beings who tend to rely on emotions to make decisions, you can explicitly consider your emotional response when making this decision.

If you have many debts with similar interest rates and terms, consideration should be given to prioritizing the repayment of callable debts (because the lender can modify the terms at any time) and secured debts (because if you don't pay, the lender can repossess their security). Crunch the numbers so you understand the math, and then determine how your life would be impacted if a callable loan was called or if you were to fall behind on secured-loan payments. With that information, you can make a decision that is in your best interests, not the bank's.

[Myth #9]

CASH IN YOUR RRSP TO PAY OFF DEBT

*Bankruptcy is always a bad idea, so if you have money
in a retirement account, use that to repay your debts.*

Conventional Wisdom

Retirement Accounts Are for Retirement

On the surface, this bit of conventional wisdom makes sense: if you
have savings or investments, you should liquidate them to repay your
debts. This is particularly the case when your investments are earning a low rate of return and the balance owing on your credit cards,
for example, is subject to a 20 percent interest rate. It's a no-brainer.
Or is it? The answer depends on the type of investments you have and
the impact of liquidating those investments.

Before I go on, let me just say that I'm not an expert in non-
Canadian investments, so I won't attempt to explain American IRAs,
401(k)s, or any other non-Canadian investment vehicle. If you have
any such investments, do some research or talk to your advisor

for more information, and consider as an example how it works in Canada, as it may help you make your decision.

In Canada, if you have a massive amount of unsecured debt and you are considering a consumer proposal or bankruptcy, it often makes no sense to cash in your retirement accounts. Let's look at an example:

> Orville lost his job and then got sick. During that time, he used his cred-it cards to survive. He's now back to work, but he owes $50,000 on his credit cards, and with their high interest rate, he has no hope of ever paying them off. He has $10,000 in a LIRA from an old employer and he has another $10,000 in an RRSP. He is considering cashing them both in to pay down his credit cards and give himself some "breathing room."

There are a number of issues with Orville's suggested approach. First, you can't simply "cash in" a locked-in retirement account (LIRA). Each province has rules governing LIRAs, because a LIRA is meant to be for your retirement, and so the regulators don't want you cashing them in whenever you feel the need. In Ontario, if you want to cash in a LIRA prior to retirement, you must make a hardship application to the Pension Commission of Ontario, and they will allow you to withdraw a lump sum of money only if you can prove hardship. Having a lot of debt does not meet their definition of a hardship, so it's unlikely Orville will qualify for a lump-sum withdrawal from his LIRA under the hardship provisions. (Hardship may include being behind on your rent or mortgage payments and facing imminent eviction, or being in need of incurring medical expenses in order to save your life. Consumer debts generally don't count.)

Second, even if Orville did qualify, there are tax consequences to withdrawing funds from a LIRA or an RRSP. The funds become income and you are required to pay tax. If you withdraw substantial funds, your income increases and you may move up into a higher tax bracket, so it's possible that you could lose half of your funds to the tax man. The $10,000 Orville has in his RRSP and in his LIRA (which is just a fancy RRSP) could easily become $5,000 each, after paying the tax.

Third, Orville has $50,000 in debts, so even if he could get up to $20,000 out of his retirement accounts, he would still have $30,000 in debts, which is more debt than he can handle. So what should Orville do? Before I answer that question, let's explore the law.

Seizable Assets

Orville should be concerned with assets that can be seized. What's a seizable asset? Any asset that is not otherwise exempt from seizure. The most common example would be your house (if you don't pay your mortgage, the mortgage holder will seize your house) or a car (if you don't pay your car loan).

In Canada, it is virtually impossible for a creditor (like a credit card company) to force you to liquidate a locked-in retirement account. That's what "locked-in" means: it can't easily be unlocked. So, even if Orville stops paying his credit cards and they sue him, it is unlikely that the court will require him to liquidate his registered accounts.

Even if Orville were to go bankrupt, it is unlikely that he would lose his LIRA or RRSP. A LIRA is locked-in, so it is not seizable in a bankruptcy.

The rules for RRSPs in Canada are slightly different. Under provisions of the *Bankruptcy and Insolvency Act*, if you go bankrupt, your trustee can seize only the contributions you have made to your RRSP in the twelve months before the bankruptcy. Let's see how this would play out for Orville.

Orville contributes $100 per month to his RRSP via an automatic RRSP deposit at his bank. So, if Orville goes bankrupt, the Licensed Insolvency Trustee administering his bankruptcy estate would expect to receive the contributions Orville made in the last twelve months, which in Orville's case would be $1,200.

In this example, if Orville was to go bankrupt, he would not lose the entire $10,000 in his RRSP; he would lose only $1,200 (his contributions in the last twelve months).

As a Licensed Insolvency Trustee, I have administered thousands of personal bankruptcies in my career and, despite the rules, I can tell you that it is very unusual for a trustee to be entitled to seize twelve months of contributions from an RRSP (for the benefit of the creditors). Why? Because, for example, if Orville knew that he was in financial trouble and was starting to consider bankruptcy, he would likely stop contributing to his RRSP. Even if he wasn't considering bankruptcy, his high debt payments would put a strain on his cash flow, so the shortage of cash would cause him to stop his RRSP contributions. A common scenario is for a debtor to see me about filing bankruptcy a few months after they have stopped contributing, and if they wait a few more months before actually filing bankruptcy, there may be only a few months' worth of contributions in the RRSP for me to seize.

Here's my point: it is unlikely that you will lose your RRSP in a bankruptcy and, therefore, it may not be in your best interests to cash in an RRSP to service your debts as an alternative to bankruptcy.

A Debt-Reduction Strategy When You Have Assets

So what should you do if you have a lot of debt and you have some assets? First, consider your unregistered, seizable assets. You won't likely lose your LIRA in a bankruptcy, but you will lose the money in your unregistered investments. If you have enough money in unregistered investments to pay your debts (after taxes on liquidation), then liquidating those investments to pay your debts makes sense. In a bankruptcy you will lose the investments anyway, so it makes sense to cash them in, pay your debts, and avoid bankruptcy.

What is an unregistered investment that you will lose in a bank-ruptcy? Here are the most common examples:

- Tax-Free Savings Account (TFSA)
- Registered Education Savings Plan (RESP), although the rules are different in each province and the math is somewhat com-plicated, so expert advice is required to crunch the numbers
- Investment accounts through your stock broker or financial advisor (unless they are registered retirement accounts)
- Bank accounts (a Licensed Insolvency Trustee doesn't care if you have a small amount of money in your bank account; but if you have a substantial amount, that's a problem for you)
- Contributions to your RRSP in the last twelve months

If you have assets and debts, do the math. If you can cash in some or all of your unregistered investments, pay the taxes owing, and still generate enough cash to repay your debts, that may be a good strat-egy. (Note: Even unregistered accounts may attract taxes when you liquidate them. For example, if you own shares in a company that have increased in value, there may be capital gains taxes owing when you sell, so again, professional advice is prudent before making a decision.)

If you have assets like a car, a boat, or a house, selling those as-sets may also be a good strategy. The rules regarding what happens to a car, boat, or house in a bankruptcy are complicated and vary from province to province and state to state, so again, professional advice is essential.

In Orville's case, if he waits until twelve months have elapsed since he last contributed to his RRSP, it is likely that he could file bankruptcy and not lose his RRSP or his LIRA. So, for Orville, going bankrupt to discharge his debts may be a good strategy.

Or it may be a crazy strategy. When deciding whether or not to go bankrupt it's not as simple as asking, "How much is in my retirement account, and what are my debts?" There are a number of other factors to consider, including:

- Other assets
- Monthly income (in a bankruptcy, the more you make, the more you pay)
- Potential windfalls (like an inheritance) that you may receive during a bankruptcy
- The impact a bankruptcy may have on your future ability to borrow
- Whether or not you can service the debts on your own

Conventional wisdom says, "Sell your stuff, pay off your debts, don't go bankrupt." Sometimes conventional wisdom is correct. If you would lose those assets anyway in a bankruptcy, the conventional way of thinking makes sense.

Practical Advice: Bankruptcy May Be Preferable to Cashing in Retirement Accounts

If you have more debts than you can ever hope to repay even if you do cash in your assets, and if you have registered assets that you wouldn't lose in a bankruptcy—and if the negative implications of a bankruptcy (like the difficulty of borrowing in the future) are not a big deal for you—a bankruptcy or a consumer proposal may be a good strategy.

Although bankruptcy may appear to be an excessively drastic step for you to take, in many cases it makes more sense than cashing in your retirement accounts in an effort to reduce or pay off your debts. Retirement accounts, as the name implies, are for your retirement, so cashing them in to repay debt is not as simple as it sounds. It has negative tax consequences and it impairs your retirement, so it is often not a sensible strategy.

Your situation is unique. Get professional advice from a Licensed Insolvency Trustee to analyze your specific circumstance and make a decision that is in your best interests, regardless of what may be suggested by conventional wisdom.

[Myth #10]

PAYDAY LOANS ARE A SHORT-TERM FIX FOR A TEMPORARY PROBLEM

Personal finance experts vilify payday loans as the most expensive form of borrowing, but they serve a need, particularly for the working class who don't have access to conventional banking services.

Conventional Wisdom

The Real (Very High) Cost of Payday Loans

Other than a loan shark, a payday loan is the most expensive form of borrowing. As of 2017 in Ontario, Canada, the maximum a payday loan lender can charge is $18 for every $100 borrowed. (The Ontario government has proposed lowering the maximum borrowing cost to $15 per $100 by 2018.) That cost of "$18 on a hundred" may appear to translate into 18 percent interest, but it's actually much higher than that, because that $18 is paid over a period much shorter than one year. As the name implies, a payday loan is designed to be repaid on your next payday; so if you get paid in two weeks, you are paying the costs of the loan in two weeks, not a full year.

Take the case of a borrower who borrows $100 and repays it two weeks later. If he repeats this process all year, that's twenty-six loans. He's borrowing only $100 each time, but he pays $18 x 26, or $468, in interest and other charges. The math is simple: $468 in costs on a biweekly $100 loan is an annual interest rate of 468 percent. That's the problem with payday loans: extremely high interest.

On that basis, payday loans are evil and should be outlawed, right? Continuing with this line of thinking, only a very unsophisticated, and probably desperate, borrower would get a payday loan; and presumably it's low-income people who get payday loans, so it's a travesty that these "legalized loan sharks" even exist, right? Perhaps. But let me present the other side of the story.

We assume that payday loans are very expensive because we compare 468 percent annual interest to a mortgage that has an annual interest rate in the single digits. On that basis, it is very expensive, but there are other ways to view interest. The interest a borrower pays can be viewed as the fee to "rent" the money they are borrowing. That's essentially what interest is: a rental fee. The borrower doesn't get to keep the money permanently; they rent it for a period of time and then return it. So if interest is rent, what does it cost to rent other items?

Try this experiment: go online and find out what it costs to rent a car. I tried it with a few different major car rental companies and found that the results were similar, although your results may vary, based on the time of year, the type of car you pick, your age, and other factors.

I selected a base-model compact car. The two-week rental rate, if I were to pay for it when I picked up the car, was $825. There were discounts available if I were to prepay or had a bonus code. Obviously, in addition to the base rental rate, I would pay for fuel and insurance. I then priced what it would cost to purchase that make of car: it was approximately $28,000, without all the fancy extras.

Now for the math: If I rented that same car every two weeks for a year, I would pay $825 x 26 = $21,450. The annual rental cost of $21,450 divided by the purchase price of $28,000 is the equivalent of 77 percent interest per year. Compared to a mortgage, that's a very high rate of interest.

Yes, I realize this is an imperfect example. The value of a car depreciates, so a car that was worth $28,000 at the start of the year is worth less at the end of the year. However, it's also likely that the car rental company buys cars in bulk and therefore gets a discount, and they likely also know the perfect time to sell the car so that they can recover a significant amount of their original cost. In my example, I rented the car for two weeks (just like with a payday loan), so a shorter- or longer-term rental would yield different results.

So what does this prove? The payday loan people would tell you that it proves that payday loans are not as costly as they initially appear. If you get a payday loan only infrequently, the few dollars you pay in interest is not that different than the few dollars you pay to rent a car infrequently. This argument makes some sense, on the assumption that payday loan–borrowing is an infrequent occurrence. Unfortunately though, for many, payday loan–borrowing is a regular occurrence.

Payday Loans Are a Symptom, Not the Problem

So who uses payday loans? My firm hired a well-known polling company to do a study of residents of Ontario[1], and we discovered that:

- 83 percent of payday loan users had other outstanding loans at the time of their last payday loan.

---

1. *www.hoyes.com/blog/payday-loans-a-symptom-of-a-bigger-problem-study/*

- 48 percent of payday loan users said they seek a short-term/ payday loan due to the amount of debt they carry.
- 46 percent of those who used a payday loan in the twelve months prior to the poll agree that a short-term/payday loan made it easier to keep up with debt repayments.
- The average non–mortgage debt owing at the time they took out a payday loan was $13,207, and for frequent users their total unsecured debt was $17,501.
- More than half of all users (55 percent) take out more than one payday loan in twelve months and, of those, 45 percent say their debt load increased post–payday loan, with only 14 percent saying their debt load decreased.
- Almost three in four (72 percent) payday loan users explored other lending sources before taking out a payday loan.
- 60 percent of those who took out a payday loan in the previous twelve months agreed that a payday/short-term loan was their last resort after exhausting all other options.
- 23 percent said they had maxed out their credit cards as a reason for seeking a payday loan.

The poll findings make it clear: You don't generally get a payday loan to "tide you over until payday." It's not actually a temporary fix to a temporary problem. As 60 percent of respondents said, a payday loan is a last resort after exhausting all other options. This is sad, for two reasons.

Most obviously, it's sad because you are in a precarious financial condition if you exhaust all other options and are left with a form of borrowing that will cost you 468 percent in annual interest. But payday loans are potentially the most damaging, in a psychological sense, because borrowers perceive their situation as helpless. They have exhausted all other options. None of us likes to be scared or apprehensive, but is there a worse feeling than helplessness?

Of my clients who have payday loans when they go bankrupt, the average client has more than three of them at the time they go bankrupt. They feel helpless and believe that they have no choice but to keep borrowing from one payday lender to another in order to stay afloat. When I ask my clients why they got a payday loan, I typically get a story like Martin's:

> Cash is always tight for Martin, so he often uses credit cards and cash advances from his line of credit to survive. At one point he was maxed out on his credit cards and line of credit and then was off work for a week, so his pay was lower than usual. He knew he would be $500 short for his rent, which was due on the first of the month, so he got a payday loan to cover the rent.

This is a very typical story, and every time I hear it my reaction is always the same: do the math. Rent is due on the first of the month and your next pay is on the fifth, so you are getting a payday loan for $500 for five days. If it costs $18 per hundred, that's $90, so you have to pay back $590 five days later. (Paying $90 for five days on $500 is the equivalent of a 1,314 percent interest rate, but let's not go there.)

Martin might tell me, "But I didn't have the money, and my rent was due; I had no other options."

And to that I would respond, "Why didn't you tell your landlord that you are very sorry but you won't be able to pay your rent until the fifth?"

Think about it. Would your landlord evict you for being five days late? In most provinces and states, that's not legal; you must give a tenant reasonable notice before you evict him or her, and five days is probably not reasonable. So, on the fifth, you bring the landlord his money, you promise it won't happen again, and you make sure that you set aside money from your next pay to cover the rent. But wait, you say, what happens if Martin is off work for longer than a week, how could he pay his rent on the fifth? Good point, but if he is off work for an extended period of time, he won't be able to pay his payday loan either, so that's not the critical component in his decision.

My point is this: you always have options. They may not be great options, but you always have more than one, and in most cases at least one of the options is better than getting a short-term, high-interest loan. If you need a payday loan to cover your rent until your next payday, talk to your landlord and pay him on your next payday, and then work on a system to set aside money so it doesn't happen again. If you end up paying $590 to repay your $500 loan, you are now $90 short for your next rent payment, so the payday loan didn't help you, it actually made your situation worse.

Here's another scary number: of my clients who go bankrupt owing money on a payday loan, the highest amount owed on payday loans is by seniors (debtors aged sixty or older), who owed on average almost $3,600 on their payday loans.[1] Why would seniors, many of whom are retired, be getting a payday loan? For the same reason as everyone else: They perceive that they have no other options. They are letting their emotions overrule their rational mind. In many cases, they are helping their adult children and they don't want to admit that they don't have the money to help them out, so they get a payday loan. But they have options. They can tell their adult children, "Sorry, I'm on a fixed income and I can't help you financially, but I'm happy to help in other ways, like looking after your kids some days."

Payday loans are an issue, but they are not the real problem. The real problem is high debt levels. If you have no other debt, you don't need to resort to a high-interest payday loan. You have other options. You can get a line of credit or a credit card. But if you already have several different kinds of debt and are maxed out on them, you believe you have no other options to get ready cash. And that's when you begin to think that payday loans are a viable option.

---

1. www.joedebtor.ca/paydayloans

Practical Advice: Be Creative, Find Other Options

So what's the solution? Unfortunately, it's not as simple as saying, "Live within your means; don't borrow money." If you have a job that barely covers your food and rent, it's very difficult to have savings to tide you over when your pay gets interrupted.

This is real life. For many people there is no obvious, easy solution. The best advice I can offer is this: You may have more control over your financial situation than you realize. You most likely do have better options than a payday loan, but you may need to use some creative thinking to come up with them. A payday loan shouldn't even be an option, because instead of relieving your situation by tiding you over until your next payday, a payday loan will put you even further into the hole, possibly for a very long time.

Before you resort to a payday loan and put yourself on the never-ending hamster wheel, consider all other possibilities. If you are short on rent, talk to your landlord. Talk to friends and family. If you are behind on your hydro bill, make a partial payment and catch up the next time you get paid. Do whatever you legally can to avoid getting a payday loan because, in simple terms, you can't afford to pay back a payday loan.

[Myth #11]

THERE IS GOOD DEBT AND BAD DEBT

Money borrowed to purchase an asset, like a house,
is good debt. Money borrowed for consumption, like
taking a vacation, is bad debt.

Conventional Wisdom

Is It That Simple?

Conceptually, the idea is easy to understand: If you borrow to buy an asset that appreciates in value, this borrowing is "good" debt. You can pay off the loan, and you're left with an asset that is worth more than you paid for it. Makes sense. If you borrow money to go on a vacation, at the end of the vacation you have nothing tangible. You don't have a house, you have only debt. This debt is bad. Makes sense. However, I believe that conventional wisdom is wrong on this point. As with most aspects of life, debt cannot be easily categorized as either good or bad.

A conventional story might go like this:

Joe buys a house for $400,000. He's able to make a $50,000 down payment, so he gets a mortgage for $350,000, at an interest rate of 4 percent, amortized over twenty-five years. His monthly payment is $1,841.07, so over the life of the mortgage he pays $552,321. Twenty-five years later, Joe sells his house for $800,000. He makes a profit of $247,679, proving that getting the mortgage was "good debt."

It's a nice story. Joe made money. Debt is good. But I can change the story to make it an example proving the opposite point:

Joe buys a house, loses his job, and has to sell the house at a loss.

In this case, was it good debt? In hindsight, no. Joe should have rented.

Here's the simple truth: Debt is neither good nor bad. Debt is a tool, just like fire. Is fire good or bad? A fire in the fireplace on a cold winter night is good, but a fire that burns down your house is bad. It's the same fire; it's how it is used that determines the outcome.

To make a moral judgment about debt, we must use hindsight. We must wait twenty-five years to see what the house sold for to determine if it was a good investment. We must wait to see if the fire stays in the fireplace or escapes and burns down the house. Without the benefit of hindsight, you cannot determine the impact of your debt.

Who Cares? I Just Want to Buy That House

So why even have this debate? Why does it matter if debt is good or bad? It matters because we allow our feelings about debt to influence our financial decisions, just as we use emotions to make most decisions. And so, if I believe that having a mortgage is good debt, I am more likely to get a mortgage to buy a house than I would be if I believe that a mortgage is bad (or neither good nor bad).

The real estate bubble in the United States that led up to the real estate crash and credit crisis of 2008 was fueled by mortgages. Ever-increasing house prices in Toronto and Vancouver in 2013, 2014, 2015, and 2016 were fueled by speculation encouraged by low mortgage interest rates. Real estate speculators with big mortgages believe mortgages are good debt, and they get caught up in the emotional high of the expectation of future profit and don't stop to consider the downside of a big mortgage.

If I believe that a house is an investment and will always go up in value, then I would think it logical to get as large a mortgage as possible and buy as expensive a house as possible, because it's a growing investment. I would consider the mortgage to be good debt because the more of it I have, the more money I will make. It's simple leverage. Contrast this with an alternate belief: mortgage debt is bad debt. If I believe mortgage debt is bad debt, I will either not buy a house or choose to buy a small house rather than a big one to minimize my mortgage.

Your moral beliefs influence your emotions, which in turn influence real-life decisions. If I believe debt is good, I will acquire more of it. It's as simple as that.

If How We Feel About Debt Shouldn't Govern Our Decisions, What Should?

Instead of approaching a debt decision as a good or bad moral decision, approach it as a math problem and use reason and thinking to solve it. Start with three questions:

Question 1: Can I afford the payments? This is a good place to start. If I buy that house, what will I be paying each month in mortgage payments (and all of the other costs associated with home ownership)? If I finance that car, what will it cost me every month?

Notice how a math question is different than a moral question. If you subjectively believe that you need a car so you can find a better job, the car loan becomes "good debt," regardless of the facts. If you approach it as a math question, it's a much different decision. You must use facts to support your decision. So, do the math.

You can take the bus to work for $100 per month, although it would take you an extra hour per day compared with how long it would take you to drive. You can finance a car, although it would cost you an extra $1,000 per month in car payments, gas, insurance, maintenance, and parking. Making your decision based on the math is easy: Is saving an hour a day of commuting time worth $1,000 per month to you? If it is, finance the car. If it isn't, perhaps you should find a less expensive car, or take the bus. The numbers are the numbers, so use the math as your starting point for making a decision about whether or not to acquire debt in any given situation.

Question 2: Will I profit from the debt? The "good debt" religion says that borrowing to buy an asset that will go up in value is a prudent financial decision. So, do the math. What is the house likely to be worth in one year, or five years, or whenever it is you're likely to sell it? No one can predict the future, but you can make a rough guess by looking at historical house prices in the neighborhood over the last twenty or thirty years. If house prices over a thirty-year period went up by slightly more than the rate of inflation, then you can take a guess at where they will be in the future.

Your guess will more than likely be wrong, because you can't predict the rate of inflation or future demographic trends, or whether some other external factor will increase or decrease real estate prices. But the exercise will help you determine how much the value of your house must increase in value to make it a good investment. If the prices have historically increased by 2 percent a year, and with your mortgage payments you need your house to increase in value by 10 percent a year, it's probably not a good investment.

Considering buying stocks on margin? Well, stocks are an investment, correct? Therefore, using margin (a loan from your stock broker) to buy stocks must be a good investment, right? In other words, margin debt must be good debt. Perhaps, but only if the stocks go up. Which brings us to the final, and most important, question.

Question 3: What's the risk? How risky is the debt? There's a risk that the stock will go down in value, but there is an even more basic risk: will you be able to make the payments?

Let's assume the house you're interested in is a good deal, you can get a good interest rate on the mortgage, and the house is in a good neighborhood, so it may go up in value. You do the math and calculate that you can easily cover the payments, assuming your life continues as it is. But what's the risk that you lose your job, or get sick, or get divorced, or for some reason are unable to make the payments? Then what?

If you lost your job tomorrow, would you have enough money in savings to cover all of your expenses until you go back to work? If you got sick for an extended period of time, do you have sufficient sick benefits to keep the lights on? These are important considerations when you are thinking of taking on a new debt. Instead of asking yourself, "Is this good debt or bad debt?" ask, "What's the risk that I won't be able to repay this debt?"

Using math and logic to make financial decisions helps lessen the influence that our perception of morality has on our decisions. Although let me be clear: I'm not against morality. In fact, I'm all for it. You and I should always do what's morally right. What I object to is attempting to assign moral characteristics to non-moral concepts. For example, is a tree good or bad? Are clouds in the sky good or bad? I'm not a philosopher, so I don't know the answers to those questions, and I don't care. Debt is the same thing; it is an amoral construct, neither good nor bad. It's a tool, so what matters is how you use it.

Practical Advice: Debt Is a Tool— Use It Only if It Fits the Task

Don't think in terms of good debt or bad debt, because assigning a moral dimension to debt may lead you to an incorrect decision. If you think mortgage debt is good, you will buy a big house. If you think all debt is bad, you will rent. You may be lucky enough to make the financial decision that's right for you despite your faulty reasoning skills, but you don't want to rely on luck when it comes to making such a big decision.

How should you view debt? Debt should be viewed as a tool, just as you would view a hammer. A hammer is neither good nor bad; all that matters is how you use it. The goal is to view debt as a tool, crunch the numbers, and make an informed decision. Don't simply follow the crowd and end up floating from one bad financial decision to another. Think for yourself, ask the right questions, and make the decision that's right for your situation.

[Myth #12]

BANKRUPTCY IS THE EASY WAY OUT

You borrowed the money; you should pay it back.

Conventional Wisdom

Bankruptcy Is Sometimes the Best Strategy

A significant percentage of personal finance experts (particularly Americans with nationally syndicated radio shows) espouse a simple opinion: "Debt is bad. You caused your debt mess, so to 'save your soul' you must 'pull yourself up by your bootstraps' and pay off your debt. Get a second job, move back in with your parents, give up everything, and do whatever else it takes, for as long as it takes, to pay off your debt."

If only life were that simple.

I will begin this chapter by repeating what I said at the start of this book: Everyone is biased. Personal finance experts want to sell you their books and courses; they want you to spend the next ten years buying their products that teach you how to get out of debt. I, too, am biased. I am a Licensed Insolvency Trustee. I am licensed by the federal government of Canada to administer consumer proposals and personal bankruptcies. If no one ever goes bankrupt, I would be out of business. From this statement you might surmise that I am not opposed to using bankruptcy as a strategy to deal with debt, and you would be correct.

So who is right? Should you pay your debts, no matter how long it takes, or should you "take the easy way out" and go bankrupt? The answer, as with all decisions in life, depends on your unique circumstances.

Why Some Say Bankruptcy Is Morally Wrong

The argument against bankruptcy is based on a simple belief: You are the cause of your own misfortune. You ended up where you are because you lived a lifestyle far above your means, spending too much, and you used debt to do it. Your financial troubles are your fault, and the only way to "save your soul" from the problems you have caused is to correct your behavior, live right, and fight your way out of debt. If spending too much caused your problems, the solution seems simple: Spend less—a lot less.

David Bach is the author of the *Finish Rich* book series, and he is credited with popularizing the concept of the "latte factor," which he explains on his website as such:

> The Latte Factor® is based on the simple idea that all you need to do to finish rich is to look at the small things you spend your money on every day and see whether you could redirect that spending to yourself. Putting aside as little as a few dollars a day for your future rather than spending it on little purchases such as lattes, bottled water, fast food, cigarettes, magazines and so on, can really make a difference between accumulating wealth and living paycheck to paycheck.[1]

---

1. *www.finishrich.com/lattefactor/*

I don't disagree with Bach's basic premise: spend less, and you will have more money to use to deal with your debts or put toward your savings. Makes sense. I also agree that, for some people, their financial problems are caused by spending excessively on things like lattes, bottled water, fast food, and cigarettes.

If you are using your credit card to buy these "wasteful" items, it could be argued that it is morally wrong to go bankrupt and not pay your debts. By not paying your debts, you're forcing the credit card company to pass on these losses to their other customers. Credit card fees go up and merchants pass their increased costs on to their customers in the form of higher prices, so it hurts everyone. That's right, by not paying for your latte you are increasing costs for everyone else, which is morally wrong. This line of reasoning seems plausible, but the facts don't support the notion that lattes are causing all of our debt problems; and, as we will see in the next section, whether or not declaring bankruptcy is a morally correct option does not depend on your latte consumption.

Debt: The Real Numbers

Every two years my firm, Hoyes, Michalos & Associates Inc., analyzes the data we are required to collect from everyone who files a consumer proposal or bankruptcy with us. We call it our *Joe Debtor* study, and it paints a picture of the average person who becomes insolvent.[1] Our average client has just under $53,000 in unsecured debt at the time he or she files their bankruptcy or consumer proposal. Unsecured debt includes credit cards, bank loans, payday loans, student loans, and taxes, but does not include secured debts like car loans and mortgages.

So here's the key question: how many lattes do you have to put on your credit card to incur $53,000 in debt? If a latte costs $3, you could buy 17,667 of them for your $53,000. If you buy one a day, for $53,000 you can buy one latte a day for over forty-eight years. The

---

1. *www.joedebtor.ca*

average age of our bankrupt client is forty-four years old. So how is it possible that in forty-four years the average bankrupt person can buy forty-eight years' worth of lattes? It would appear that lattes do not cause personal bankruptcy.

Yes, I realize that I'm presenting a silly example. I realize that if you did use your credit card to buy a latte each morning, you would be incurring interest on your purchases, so your credit card balance would get to $53,000 a lot faster than forty-eight years. I also realize that for the first eighteen or twenty years of your life you probably didn't have a credit card and probably weren't buying lattes. But my example is no more fanciful than the examples given by the personal finance experts. "Give up your latte," they say, "and you will be a millionaire."

Okay, I can do that math. Let's assume that every time you go to the coffee shop you buy a latte and a donut or some other tasty treat, and you spend $10 each visit; and you sometimes go more than once a day, so it adds up to $100 per week, which is $5,200 per year. Now let's assume that instead of spending that $100 at the coffee shop every week, you save it; and you earn 10 percent interest on those savings and pay no tax on the earnings. With those assumptions, in less than thirty-two years you will have a million dollars. See, your latte is costing you a million dollars! Cut out the lattes and you will be a millionaire! But this is also a fanciful example. Do you really spend $100 a week lattes and baked goods? Can you really earn 10 percent on your savings?

Let's look at a more realistic example. What if you spend $5 per day, five days per week? If you gave up your fancy-coffee habit and saved the money instead in a savings account that paid only 1 percent in interest, then even with no taxes owing, after thirty-two years you would have less than $50,000 in your savings account. Not exactly the million-dollar plan, is it?

I agree that we should keep our expenses to a minimum, but I don't believe that lattes are the cause of all of our financial problems. So what is the cause of financial problems that often lead to bankruptcy? Based on our *Joe Debtor* studies, the common causes of insolvency are exactly what you would expect: job loss, medical problems, and divorce. Here's one such story:

> Alan had a good job. He worked hard and saved money. He had a decent down payment when he bought his house. Then his employer went out of business and Alan was out of a job. He found another job, but it took three months to find it, and he had to deplete some of his savings while he was unemployed. His new job doesn't pay as much as his old job, and it's a longer commute, so his transportation expenses are now higher. Shortly after starting his new job, Alan got sick. Because he was still in his probationary period, he didn't qualify for medical benefits, so while he was off sick, he depleted the rest of his savings and began using his line of credit and credit cards to pay for medication, his mortgage payments, and other living expenses. During this time, his mother was placed in a nursing home due to her medical issues, and Alan, as the only child, helped with her expenses. He used credit to make those payments. Eventually, Alan became unable to service his debt and one of the creditors started garnisheeing his wages.

So what should Alan do? Just suck it up and pay his debts? Sure, that would be great, but his income is now reduced due to the wage garnishment, and he simply doesn't have enough income to make his debt payments every month. Alan has to make a choice: He can keep struggling, stop supporting his mother, and live with the wage garnishment, or he can file bankruptcy, eliminate his debts, and without the debt payments he will be able to make ends meet.

Real life is not simple. It's not as simple as saying, "Just pay your debts." For some people, bankruptcy is not only the correct strategy, it's also the only logical strategy. It's easy for someone with a good job and lots of money in the bank to debate the morality of bankruptcy, but when you don't have enough cash flow to meet your monthly expenses, "morality" is not the first word that comes to mind. The word is "survival," and it becomes your most important objective.

Some People Can't Pay Their Debts

Yes, you should pay your debts, but the devil is in the details. Let's take the example of someone who has total debts of $26,500. A financial expert would advise him or her to make their minimum monthly payment on all of their debts, and then devote any extra money to the highest interest rate debt. Here's what the financial "expert" would tell this person:

> Your debt is divided among your credit cards, and the interest rate on each of the cards is 19 percent per year, so your total interest charge in the first month is $420. If you can find $800 in your budget to commit to a debt-repayment plan, in the first month you pay $420 in interest, and the remaining $380 is applied to principal. Each month, as your principal is reduced, more of your $800 is applied to reduce the principal. With this plan, it will take only forty-eight months to be debt-free.

This plan works great if:

- you can find $800 per month in your budget for debt payments, and
- you can keep at it for forty-eight months (which is four years).

If you have a high-paying job and can afford $800 per month, and if you can avoid getting laid off or injured or otherwise unemployed at any point in the next four years, this plan works. Unfortunately though, many of the people I work with don't have $800 to spare per month. In fact, while 78 percent of the people who file a bankruptcy or consumer proposal have a job, the average net income of all insolvent debtors in our study was $2,377 per month, and with this income they must service their average unsecured debt of almost $53,000.[1]

In simple terms, the average person who goes bankrupt or files a consumer proposal has twice as much debt as in the example above,

---

1. *www.hoyes.com/blog/joedebtor/who-is-the-average-joe-debtor/*

so if we keep the math simple and assume they have $800 per month for debt repayment, it would take twice as long, about eight years, to get out of debt on their own. But wait! If the interest charges were $420 per month for the person with $26,500 in debt, the person with $53,000 in debt would have minimum payments of over $840 per month. If they have only $800 per month for debt repayment, they have a problem. They can't even make their interest payments, so they have no chance to start actually paying down debt in a meaningful way.

Sound bad? It gets worse. Most credit cards require you to pay the interest each month as well as make a payment against principal, of perhaps 3 percent of the balance owing. So, on $26,500 in credit card debt, they would be required to make a monthly payment of 3 percent of the outstanding balance (just under $800), plus the interest (about $420), for a total payment in the first month of over $1,200. If all he or she can afford is $800 per month, they cannot mathematically satisfy the credit card company.

Of course, I have also ignored the obvious: how can someone earning $2,377 per month pay $800 per month in debt payments? This leaves just $1,577 to pay rent, food, transportation, and other living expenses, which would be very difficult. I also ignored another obvious point: my typical client has $53,000 in debt, not $26,500, so when you double the amount of debt, and double the required payments, it becomes even more obvious that if you have more debt than you can service with your income, a strategy of more than "skip the lattes" is necessary.

Practical Advice: Pay Down Debt or Go Bankrupt?

So here's my suggested strategy: To start with, I absolutely agree that you should review your spending and look for ways to cut costs in order to free up cash for debt payments. If you can free up enough cash to repay your debts in a reasonable time, that is absolutely the correct strategy. What is a reasonable time frame? That depends on your age and financial stability. If you are relatively young and work in a stable job, you may be able to devote three or four years to repaying debt. However, if you are closer to retirement, or your job is not secure, or your income bounces up and down, a long-term plan may not be possible.

If you don't have the cash flow to repay your debts in a reasonable period of time, the prudent approach is to consider other alternatives. Other alternatives may include getting help from family or considering bankruptcy or a consumer proposal. You can deal with some problems yourself, while other problems require professional assistance. I can fill my car tires up with air, but I don't attempt to fix my own transmission. For large problems I consult an expert. The key, of course, is to know whether your debts are small enough that you can pay them on your own or if they are large enough that the only way to secure your financial future, for you and your family, is to get professional help. Crunch the numbers to determine the answer in your unique situation, and if you can't crunch the numbers on your own, get professional help.

PART 3
REAL ESTATE

[Myth #13]

A HOUSE IS A GREAT INVESTMENT

*Over a long time period, house prices always go up,
so the foundation of any good financial plan is home
ownership; it's a great investment, and you can't lose.*

Conventional Wisdom

What Is an Investment?

Let's start with a simple question: what is an investment? My definition of an investment is something that either:

- gives you regular income (like interest on a bond, or dividends on a stock), or
- will increase in value, so you can sell it for more than you paid for it.

By that definition, it's easy to see why buying a house is not an investment, for two obvious reasons:

1. A house does not generate income (unless it's a rental property; but in this chapter we are discussing the house you live in, not an investment property).

2. A house may not increase in value.

Let's consider each reason in more detail.

Your House Does Not Generate Income

An investment pays you money, but the house you live in does not pay you money every month. In fact, it's the opposite: you pay money out for the mortgage, property taxes, and repairs and maintenance. Using this "income" test, a house is clearly not an investment. That's why I consider a personal residence a liability, not an asset.

But wait, you say! What about a rental property? It is possible that a rental property could generate cash flow for you every month. If the rent you collect is greater than your expenses (mortgage, property taxes, maintenance, and repairs when the tenant trashes the place and you have to fix it), then yes, a rental property can be an investment as defined by cash flow. But as I said above, that's not what we are talking about. We are talking about whether or not the house you live in is an investment. The house you live in is not paying you money for the portion you are living in, so it's not an investment—unless it meets the second test, which is capital appreciation.

If you buy a house for $200,000 and sell it for $240,000, it would appear that you have earned $40,000 in profit, so on that basis it appears to be an investment. That may be true, but let's be sure we are comparing apples to apples. Let's look at an example:

> Barry and Brenda bought a house for $200,000. They lived in it and owned it for five years, then sold it for $240,000. During the time they owned the house they installed a new roof and a new furnace, did some landscaping, and renovated the kitchen and bathroom for a total cost of $50,000.

So their "profit" is actually a loss: $240,000 selling price − $200,000 purchase price − $50,000 in repairs = −$10,000. A house is not an investment. It's a consumer good, just like a toothbrush or a computer. You use it, and then you throw it away.

Throw away a house. Am I crazy? I grew up in a house that was built in 1867; obviously it wasn't "thrown away," as it is still there now, 150 years later. So what am I saying? I'm saying that, while you don't dispose of an entire house like you would a used toothbrush, a house is replaced, piece by piece, over time. Over a twenty-year period, it is likely that a house will require replacement of the roof, windows, plumbing fixtures, electrical components, carpets, flooring, furnace, air conditioning, and all appliances.

A toothbrush is not an investment, and neither is a house when you factor in the actual costs of upkeep. Barry and Brenda made the same mistake most people make: they compare the selling price of their house to the purchase price, and declare, "We made a profit," but they ignore the repair costs that they incurred to earn that profit.

Opportunity Cost

Repair costs are easy to understand, but for many homeowners it's not the obvious costs (mortgage, repairs) that make a house a poor investment, it's the opportunity cost. Opportunity cost is the cost of choosing one alternative over another. It's the cost of a lost opportunity.

You need to live somewhere, so you have a choice: rent or own. The simplistic analysis is to compare the cost of rent to the mortgage payment, leading to the conclusion that it's cheaper to own than to rent. A more sophisticated analysis includes the repair and maintenance costs and property taxes in this analysis, but the analysis is only complete if you include the opportunity cost. Take Chad's story, for instance:

Chad has a choice: rent a townhouse for $2,000 per month, or buy that same townhouse. He has $40,000 for a down payment, and if he were to purchase the townhouse his monthly carrying costs for the mortgage, property taxes, and minor repairs and maintenance would be about $1,900 per month, so Chad decides to buy the townhouse because "it's cheaper than renting."

Chad's mistake, of course, is that he forgot to consider the opportunity cost of his $40,000. If he buys the house, the $40,000 becomes his down payment. If he rents the house instead, he can invest the $40,000 and presumably earn a return on that investment. If Chad can earn a 6 percent after-tax return on his $40,000, his opportunity cost is 6 percent of $40,000, or $2,400 per year. An annual opportunity cost of $2,400 translates to $200 per month. This changes the "rent versus buy" math. Chad can rent for $2,000 per month, but he would be earning $200 per month in investment income, so his net cost to rent and to invest his down payment money is $2,000 − $200, or $1,800 per month.

By considering opportunity cost, the math changes. Instead of the $1,900 in mortgage payments being thought of as cheaper than the rent of $2,000, the $1,900 monthly mortgage payment is actually more expensive than the rent-adjusted cost of $1,800 per month.

Houses Don't Always Go Up in Value

This is the most important reason why a house is not an investment: houses can go down in value. Anyone who lived in Alberta during the oil-price correction of 2015 and 2016 understands this. Unfortunately, those who have experienced only boom times, such as anyone who owned a house in Toronto during the period from 2010 through 2016, believe that house prices always go up. This is not the case.

Here's a chart based on data from the Toronto Real Estate Board that shows average sale prices of houses in Toronto between 1983 and 2002, as reported on the Toronto Real Estate Board's Multiple Listing Service.[1]

---

1. *www.trebhome.com/market_news/market_watch/historic_stats/pdf/treb_historic_statistics.pdf* *(Retrieved December, 2016)*

Toronto MLS Average Sale Price

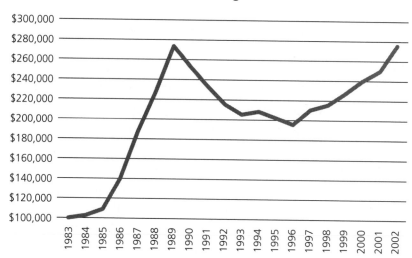

As you can see, average house prices peaked in 1989 at $273,698 and remained below that level until 2002, when the average recorded sale price was $275,231. So if you bought a house in Toronto in 1989 that represented the exact average price and then you sold it at any time over the next twelve years, you would have lost money. The bottom of the cycle happened in 1996, when the average Toronto house sold for $198,150. If you bought at the peak in 1989 and sold at the bottom in 1996, you would have owned your house for eight years and lost almost 28 percent on your "investment."

Although yes, I get it. If you bought a house in Toronto in 1984 at the average price of $102,318 and sold it in 1988 for $229,635, you more than doubled your money, with a profit of 125 percent in only four years (if you ignore the cost of interest, property taxes, repairs and maintenance, and renovations). That would have been a great "investment."

This is the key point: houses do not always go up in value. There are periods of time when they decrease in value. Whether or not you make money on real estate is largely dependent on when in the real estate cycle you buy and sell. If you buy at the peak and sell at the bottom, you lose. If you buy at the bottom and sell at the peak, you can make a lot of money.

If you are buying a house to make money, clearly your chances of profit are much greater if you "buy low and sell high." This leads to the fundamental question every real estate investor must ask themselves: Where are we in the real estate cycle? Closer to the top, or closer to the bottom? Surprisingly, this is a relatively easy question to answer. Do a Google search for historical real estate prices in your city, and your local real estate board will probably have a chart similar to the one above that shows the Toronto market in the 1980s and 1990s. Look at a long-term chart, ideally from 1980 to today. In most cities in North America, you will see peaks around 1988 and then again in the 2006-to-2008 period. Many cities in the United States experienced significant declines around the time of the credit crisis in 2008; some cities in Canada were less impacted. Regardless, with a long-term chart it is easy to see whether today's real estate prices are closer to the top or the bottom of the cycle compared with previous years.

If you did this exercise in Toronto in 1987, you would have observed modest annual increases in the early 1980s and then much more significant increases:

- 1984 + 1 percent increase
- 1985 + 7 percent increase
- 1986 + 27 percent increase
- 1987 + 36 percent increase

With results like that, what would you have predicted would happen in 1988? You could have predicted an even larger increase, perhaps 50 percent or more. In fact, in 1988 in Toronto average house prices increased by 21 percent, and then increased by another 19 percent in 1989, before beginning a seven-year period during which house prices decreased in every year but one (in 1994, when house prices increased by 1 percent, and then fell again by 3 percent and 2 percent over the next two years).

So what would you have done in 1987? Buy, because the market always goes up? Wait for a correction? No one knows the future, so there was some justification for either approach, but there was no doubt that even in 1987 the market had already experienced a significant increase, and as prices move higher the risk of a big price drop increases, so real estate was a risky investment back in 1987. What about 1989? What would you have done in 1989, at the peak of the market? I know the answer to that question because I bought a house in 1989. Oops.

I was living in a relatively small town north of Toronto at the time. I had a good job working for a large accounting firm, and the banks were eager to lend money. I found a townhouse in a complex where, a year before, a similar unit had sold for $275,000. I bought my unit for $205,000. Brilliant! Obviously the market had peaked and I was getting a great deal. Right?

Nope. The market had peaked, but that's not the same as the market bottoming. The market continued to fall, and I sold that townhouse almost eight years later for a loss of $20,000. I owned it for more than seven years and made mortgage payments and paid condo fees and property taxes that, combined, equaled more than monthly rent payments would have, and after seven years I had a loss to show for my troubles. I had made the classic mistake: I assumed that prices wouldn't drop. I was correct in understanding that the market had peaked, but I didn't envision that the market would either stagnate or fall for seven years. It did, and I lost.

Of course, timing is everything. By the summer of 2016, the units in that complex, where I had sold at a loss in 1997, were selling for over $650,000. So if I had held on for nineteen more years I would have made a big profit. But nineteen years was a long time, and living in a small townhouse in a distant city, with a family, wouldn't work for me.

So Should I Buy a House or Not?

There's one question that is a surefire litmus test to help you decide whether or not you should commit to buying a house: "Why do I want to buy a house?" Write down your answer. If the answer is, "Because a house is a great investment and houses always go up in value," you are wrong; we've already seen that they don't. If your answer is, "I have a spouse, two kids, and a dog and a cat, and it's almost impossible to find a place to rent near a good school that also allows you to have a dog and a cat," then okay, those are valid reasons for wanting to buy a house. You may be correct: in order to be near a good school and be able to have a dog and a cat, your best option may be to buy a house.

I don't object to people buying houses. We all need a place to live, and there are many advantages to owning a house. You can paint the walls whatever color you want, and you don't have to worry about the landlord selling the place and kicking you out. But owning a house is very different from *investing* in a house. I own my cellphone, but I don't consider it an investment, because I realize it won't increase in value and it will eventually require replacement. You own a house because you need a place to live, not because you expect it to increase in value. It may increase in value, which is great, but that's not why you own it.

The key point is your expectation. Do you expect the house to go up in value? If you do, you're treating your house as an investment. Why is that a problem? Because if it's an investment that you expect to go up in value, you will be tempted to buy as expensive a house as possible, to maximize your investment gains. That strategy will be a disaster if house prices fall.

By viewing your house as a consumer good, not as an investment, you can free yourself from the need to buy the most expensive house and instead focus on what is truly important to you: Is the house close to good schools? Is there a yard for your dog to run around in? Can you paint the walls your preferred shade of pale green? This approach makes sense, but this is not the process most people use when making house-buying decisions. We don't use logic. We use our emotions.

Keeping Up with the Joneses

Our emotions guide our house-buying decisions, and in many cases our emotions are driven by wanting to keep up with our friends. A house purchase is probably the most emotional purchase decision you will ever make, and this is why it is essential to realize the role that emotion is playing in your buying decision.

Have you ever visited friends at their new house and thought to yourself, "Wow, their house is great. My house looks shabby in comparison. We need to consider buying a better house"? It happens all the time, and I suspect that many house-buying decisions are a direct result of wanting to buy a house similar to, or better than, that of those in our social group. "Because my friend has a big house" is not a good reason for you to buy an expensive home.

Practical Advice: Take Emotion Out of the Equation

Don't fall into the conventional wisdom trap of assuming that whatever house you buy will be a great investment. If you are buying at the top of the regular real estate market cycle, your house may be a very poor investment.

Acknowledge that emotion guides your house-buying decision. Consciously make an effort to explore the decision rationally by crunching the numbers. When you have the cold, hard numbers in front of you, you may make a better decision.

It won't be easy. You are human, and we all use our "gut" to make decisions. But the price you pay for allowing your emotions to make your buying decision is that you may end up with a house much more expensive than you can afford. If this happens, you become "house poor" and your house becomes your greatest financial liability, as we will explore in the next two chapters. Stay tuned, we're getting to the meaty part of the most common real estate myths.

[Myth #14]

OWNING A HOUSE
GIVES YOU STABILITY

*As a renter, you are at the mercy of your landlord. If
your landlord sells the house or decides to raise the
rent or evict you, you are out on the street. If you own a
house, you control your life.*

Conventional Wisdom

A House Is an Anchor

A house can give you stability, but so can a boat anchor. If I don't
want my boat to move, an anchor is great; but if I can't pull the anchor out of the water, my boat isn't going anywhere, and so it is with
houses.

In the good old days, 150 years ago, people lived on the same
farm for their entire lives and then passed it on to their children. The
farm, and the house, gave the family stability. Fifty years ago, your
father or grandfather likely worked at the same company for his entire working career and lived in the same house for fifty years, so the

family home was a stabilizing constant. It was like a boat anchor, but that was good, because the "boat" wasn't going anywhere.

Today, life is different, as your responses to the following self-assessment test will prove.

SELF-ASSESSMENT TEST #4

1. How many people do you know who retired at age sixty-five and were employed by the same company for their entire working career?
2. What about you: how long have you worked for your current employer?
3. How many different employers have you had in your working career?
4. How many different careers have you had?

You see my point. Life today constantly changes. We are much more likely to change jobs and to move to different cities, or even countries, than we ever were in the past. But having a house, with a mortgage, makes it difficult to just pick up and move. Consider Sonya's situation:

> Sonya owns a house that she bought two years ago when she started a new job. Today the house is worth about $500,000, with a mortgage of $470,000. A head hunter has approached Sonya about a great job opportunity. She would have more responsibility and significantly higher pay if she were to accept the opportunity, but she would have to move to a new city. Sonya does the math and realizes that if she sells her house and pays the real estate commission and the penalty to break the mortgage she would, at best, break even. She doesn't want to lose her house investment, so she decides not to take the new job.

For Sonya, her house is an anchor, and it's not just because of the money. To sell her house, she would have to hire a real estate agent and put up with open houses, buyer tours on short notice, and late-night meetings with her agent to consider offers. If the real estate market is hot, great; but if it's a buyer's market and Sonya has to list the house for months to sell it, selling her house would be a real hassle. She wants to move and get on with her new career, but instead she'd be tied to her old house in her old city.

If Sonya had rented her place for the last two years instead of owning it, it's likely that she would be on a month-to-month lease, so it would be relatively easy to pick up and move. No real estate commissions, no penalties to break a mortgage. She would have a better job at higher pay and would be off on an exciting new adventure. Instead, she is stuck in her house.

So why did Sonya buy a house in the first place? Perhaps she thought it would be a good investment, but as we discussed in the last chapter, that is not always the case. If you have a ten- or twenty-year time horizon, your house is likely to go up in value; however, if you move in two years, good luck. After real estate commissions and other selling costs, it's not easy to make a profit in the short term.

Perhaps Sonya bought the house for emotional reasons. She wanted a place to call her own. That's perfectly understandable, but what's more important than a *place* to call your own is a *life* to call your own. Sonya traded her life for a house. Now, obviously Sonya is still alive, so she didn't literally trade her life for a house, but her house prevented her from living the life she wanted to live. She can't just pick up and move for a better job. She is stuck.

So what can we learn from Sonya? Before you think about buying a house, consider your timelines. What are the chances that your life will change in the next five years, requiring you to move? Is there any chance you'll be offered a job in a different city? We always assume we will stay working where we are forever, but is this likely? Does your employer provide a product or service that will never change? If you work in a hospital or a school, your job is likely to exist in the future, so there is less risk to "putting down roots." But if you work as a contract employee at a high-tech start-up, there is very little chance you will be in the same job in two years, and certainly not in five years. For you, a house might be an anchor.

Is your family situation likely to change? Your 500-square-foot bachelor-pad condo downtown is great for you as a single person working long hours, but would it be suitable if you get married and have three kids? (No, no it wouldn't.) Families grow and families shrink, so housing needs change. Having a big house in the suburbs is great when you have kids, but a big house in the suburbs is a liability once the kids have moved on.

Is your medical situation likely to change? (Yes, yes it is.) We all get older. Running up the stairs in your three-level house is no big deal when you're thirty years old; it's not so fun when you have a few more decades under your belt. A smaller bungalow near medical services would be more appropriate as you get older.

Is your social situation likely to change? As a young parent, you spend your evenings and weekends in cold hockey arenas in the winter and at football, baseball, and soccer games in the summer; and you hang out with all of the other parents at dance practice, piano lessons, and every other kid-centered activity. Once the kids are older or have moved out, your social network changes. You don't need to live close to the hockey arena; you are more interested in your proximity to good restaurants and other places where adults hang out without kids. When you become an "empty-nester," your housing requirements change accordingly.

Practical Advice: Look Ahead

Before you buy a house, consider the future. If you are likely to want or need to move to a different city for any reason in the next two years, renting is the prudent alternative. You will avoid all of the hassles, and cost, of moving. If any other aspect of your life is likely to change over the next few years, consider the impact of those changes on your housing situation. Buying a big house today for your large family may not be prudent if your children are older teenagers likely to be going off to college or otherwise moving out on their own.

This doesn't mean you should never buy a house, but you should consider all of your options and your needs over the near term. If you have three kids but one of them will be moving out next year, do you need a four-bedroom house, or will a smaller two- or three-bedroom house suffice? Can you set Kid #1 up in the basement for the next year until she moves on? How is your health? Perhaps a condo or bungalow is a better option than a three-level house.

Finally, do you want an anchor? Perhaps you do. If your family is young, having a place to put down roots for the next ten or twenty years may be the perfect plan. If it makes sense, great, do it; but buy a house only if you want, and need, an anchor.

[Myth #15]

THE BIGGER
THE MORTGAGE,
THE BETTER

*It's okay to take out a bigger mortgage, because doing
so increases your leverage, and increases your profit.*

Conventional Wisdom

The Chapter That Writes Itself

If you've read the last two chapters, you know where I'm going with
this one; so if you already know the answer, feel free to skip ahead to
the next chapter. For the rest of you, let's blow this one away.

As with many aspects of life, the conventional wisdom regarding
mortgage size is partially correct. Over a long period (ten or twenty
years), house prices historically have increased. However, there are
many examples of house prices dropping and not recovering for five
years, so if your time frame is short, there is no guarantee you will

make money on a real estate investment. Also, mortgage rates may be at a low point in the cycle now, but interest rates historically go up and down, so there is no guarantee that you will always have an attractive and affordable mortgage interest rate.

This is why I believe that it is definitely possible to have a mortgage that is too large for you in your unique circumstances. If house prices soften or interest rates increase, or both, you could be left with more mortgage debt than you can handle. You know this—this insight is not worth the price of this book, nor is it worth the sixty seconds you have already devoted to reading this chapter. However, there is one word that is worth the price of admission and is the basis for what we are about to discuss: leverage.

If you buy stocks on margin, you understand leverage. If my broker is willing to loan me money to buy stocks, I can use leverage to increase my returns. I put up $1,000 and my broker loans me $1,000, so now I can buy $2,000 worth of stock. If the stock doubles in value, I now own $4,000 worth of stock. I sell, pay back my broker the $1,000 I borrowed, and now I have $3,000, which is three times my initial investment of $1,000. That's leverage. If I hadn't bought on margin, my $1,000 would have turned into $2,000 when the stock doubled, which is still a great return, but doubling is not as great as tripling. Thanks, leverage!

Of course, leverage works both ways. If my stock declines by 50 percent, the $2,000 worth of stock I bought (my $1,000 and my broker's $1,000) is now worth $1,000. I sell, use that money to pay off my broker, and I'm left with nothing. I'm wiped out. Busted. Had I not used leverage, I would have lost "only" 50 percent, but with leverage I lost everything. Thanks, leverage.

And so it is with buying a house, except there is much more leverage! Your stock broker won't lend you anything against a penny stock; you may get 50 percent leverage on a blue chip stock. With a house, you can make a 5 percent down payment and get a mortgage for 95 percent of the purchase price. That's extreme leverage.

Just as a stock can go up or down in value, so, too, can a house. If you buy a $1-million-dollar house with a $50,000 down payment and a 95 percent mortgage, and the house goes up by 10 percent, or $100,000, you just doubled your money! You invested $50,000 and made $100,000 (assuming there is no such thing as real estate commissions or any other costs). The opposite is also true: If your house drops by a mere 5 percent, which as we discussed in the last chapter is very common, your entire down payment is gone. You are wiped out (if you sell your house).

The Appropriate Level of Leverage

Let's say your bank pre-qualifies you for a $500,000 mortgage. You decide you don't want maximum leverage, so you decide to buy a house that, along with your down payment, will require only a $475,000 mortgage. That's prudent, right? Or is it? Why did you decide on $475,000? Why not $490,000? Or $400,000?

The important question is not, "Should I max out my mortgage?" (no, too risky) but instead, "How much mortgage should I carry?" So how big is too big? How can you tell if you have more mortgage than you can handle? There are two factors to consider.

Is your monthly payment affordable?

There are a lot of percentages out there, but in truth, how much you can afford depends on your lifestyle. If you want to have a life where you can occasionally go to a restaurant or go on vacation or save for your children's education, you can't afford to overextend yourself with mortgage payments. If you live a frugal lifestyle and your desire is to own a larger home, you might be able to keep up with larger payments.

Here's the thing: No matter how much you hate it, you have to run some numbers. Make a list of your expected housing expenses before you buy a home or take on a second mortgage. If you would struggle to make your mortgage payment each month (plus your property taxes, condo fees, and other expenses), the mortgage is too big.

How much equity do you have in your house?

Equity is the cash you would get if you sold your house. To calculate your equity, take the estimated selling price of your house and subtract the mortgage balance *and* selling costs (real estate commissions, legal fees, and any penalties to break your mortgage). The difference is your equity.

Note: It is a common misconception to assume that your down payment is equal to your equity, but that is not accurate. If you buy a house with a $50,000 down payment on Monday and sell the house on Tuesday for exactly what you paid for it, you won't get your $50,000 back, because you pay real estate commissions and legal fees when you sell your house, which reduces your equity. Your equity is the actual cash you would get if you sold your house, after all expenses.

So what proportion of equity is a safe number?

Obviously the more equity you have, the better, but owning a home is not a cushion against bankruptcy. In fact, the size of your mortgage can be an added risk factor. In our most recent *Joe Debtor* study,[1] the average insolvent homeowner owed a total of $191,464 in secured mortgages. Almost one in ten (9 percent) had negative equity in their home, even before considering selling costs. Once real estate commissions and other selling costs are factored in, only 57 percent of insolvent homeowners would be able to sell their home and generate a positive net realizable value. Even for those with positive equity, the average equity available for creditors was only $20,708, or 9 percent of the average home value of $224,306. That's not much equity.

So what's the level of mortgage that is "too big"?

If your mortgage amounts to 90 percent or more of the value of your house, based on our numbers, you are at serious risk of having debt problems that may require you to file a bankruptcy or a consumer

---

1. *www.joedebtor.ca*

proposal. What is the reason for this? You have no margin for error. With only 10 percent house equity (or less) you may not be able to sell your house and cover your selling costs and "get out even."

I recommend that you crunch the numbers on your mortgage to determine if you're at risk and, if you are, take steps to pay down your mortgage faster or consider selling your house and moving to less-expensive accommodation, if possible.

It's Not Just About the Numbers

Crunching the numbers is always a good idea before you buy a house (which is why I recommended it in the last paragraph), but the numbers are only part of the story, and perhaps not the most important part. Consider this scenario:

> Raymond and Olga crunched the numbers: They know their income and they know what their costs are for food, transportation, and utilities. The difference between their inflows and outflows is what they calculated they could afford in mortgage payments, so they talked to their bank and got pre-approved for a mortgage that would have mortgage payments that they can "afford."

What a nice story. Raymond and Olga did the math and now they can buy a house, secure in the knowledge that they can afford their mortgage payments. If I were having a coffee with the happy couple, I would ask them two questions:

1. Did you consider all of your expenses? It's not just food and transportation and utilities that matter. There's also home repairs and maintenance and many other costs a new home-owner may not consider.
2. Do you have a life? If so, what does that life cost?

I remember when my wife and I were first married, in the period she fondly refers to as B.K. (Before Kids). Every Friday we would walk to our favorite restaurant. The owners knew us, so without asking they would pour her a glass of her favorite libation (I believe it was red and served in a wine glass), and we would enjoy our dinner. During our B.K. period, we lived in town, within walking distance of restaurants. At least once every week we went out for dinner and it cost us money to do that. Let's assume, for the sake of this discussion, that eating out a few times a month had cost $400 per month more than it would have cost if we had cooked food and stayed home. Now think of your own situation. Are you willing to get a mortgage that costs $400 less per month so that you have the cash flow to go out for dinner a few times a month?

You see, you can spend a dollar only once, so you have to choose, and "resource allocation" questions are not always easy. I like to go out for dinner, but I also want to live in a big house, which requires a bigger mortgage. You are the boss, so you have to decide which is more important to you: the big house, or dinner out. Of course, going out for dinner is just one example. You may want to spend your money on other things, like a vacation, or furniture for your house, or saving for your children's education. The problem with a big mortgage is that it prevents you from spending money in every other area of your life. In this sense, you are "house poor."

How to Avoid Being House Poor

You are house poor if you're spending so large a portion of your income on home ownership costs (mortgage, property taxes, etc.) that you don't have sufficient cash to spend on other priorities (savings, investments, vacations, etc.). A common measure of reasonable house costs is 35 percent of your net income.[1] If you are over that amount, you are at risk for being house poor.

There are two events that can lead to being house poor: 1) buying a house that costs more than you can afford, and 2) experiencing a

---

1. *www.moneyproblems.ca/debt-solutions-blog/5-key-spending-ratios/*

change in your financial situation (e.g., having children) after you buy the home that you could afford when you first bought it.

How does home ownership lead to financial difficulty? Let's delve deeper into the most recent *Joe Debtor* study conducted by Hoyes, Michalos & Associates Inc.[1] We analyzed over 6,000 people in Ontario who filed a consumer proposal or personal bankruptcy with us. You can read the detailed comments in our section on High-Risk Mortgages,[2] but here's a summary of some of our key findings.

Of the people in our study who filed a bankruptcy or consumer proposal, 17 percent owned a home at the time of their insolvency. This fact demonstrates that owning a home does not protect you from insolvency. What is more important, however, is that for those who become insolvent, their home mortgage is not their only debt. In fact, the reason the homeowners in our study became insolvent is because, in addition to their mortgage, they are carrying over $72,000 in unsecured debt.

Why does a homeowner owe so much on credit cards, bank loans, and other unsecured debts? I can tell you from my professional experience that, in many cases, the cost of home ownership is higher than expected, so to cover the unexpected repairs and maintenance costs, homeowners use their credit card to make ends meet. In addition, when you buy a home you need to furnish it, and that is often done by borrowing.

The data proves the point: houses are great—unless you can't afford them, then they become a significant burden that can lead to insolvency.

Older people were raised to believe that the bigger the house the better, but many younger people have a different perspective. Younger Canadians can see what has happened to their older friends and co-workers, and to their parents. They observe that, in order to afford a big house, in some cases it means you have to be "house

---

1. *www.joedebtor.ca*
2. *www.hoyes.com/press/joe-debtor/high-risk-mortgages/*

poor," and they don't want that. When you are young you want to be able to go out for dinner and drinks with friends, and maybe go on a nice vacation. You may want to get married and start a family, and this is difficult to do when a big portion of your income goes toward a mortgage payment. This may be one reason why the average age of first-time marriages continues to increase, and it's certainly why many younger people are deciding to rent instead of own—particularly in big cities, where it's a lot easier to rent and live close to work than it is to buy.

Practical Advice: Buy or Rent?

So what's the answer? Follow these three simple steps: consider all of your expenses, consider your equity, and then do the third step, which is the most important: *stress test* all of your assumptions. Perhaps you can afford the mortgage, but what happens if you lose your job or your hours are reduced at work? Do you have a sufficient emergency fund to get you through a period of unemployment? Figure out the worst-case scenario for home repairs. What would a new roof cost? A new furnace? What would it cost to repair a flood in your basement?

By stress testing the numbers and considering all options, you can make a more informed decision. This is easy to say but hard to do, because you can't predict every possible life event that could derail your home ownership plans. However, you can make reasonable guesses. Houses need repair, so build your best guesses into your estimates. You may need to move, so factor that in to your analysis. With as many facts as possible, you can make a more informed decision rather than just floating along accepting conventional wisdom and making your decisions based on that.

With all of the facts, you may decide on a smaller house with a smaller mortgage. You may even decide to eliminate the home ownership risk entirely and rent, and in many cases that is the most prudent decision. The point is, whatever you do, don't take at face value the conventional wisdom that a house is the better investment and that a bigger mortgage will pay off bigger for you in the long run. You have lots of other options, and one of them may be better for you. This is a big decision that potentially involves tying up a lot of your money and affecting your lifestyle overall—go into it with your eyes completely open.

PART 4

BUDGETING AND PLANNING

[Myth #16]

INVESTMENT EXPERTISE IS THE KEY TO GOOD MONEY MANAGEMENT

To make a budget you need a spreadsheet, a phone app, and one hour per week. To save, you need to shop the banks for the best interest rate. To prosper, you need extensive expertise in all aspects of investment.

Conventional Wisdom

Investing Is Not the Key Component of a Successful Financial Plan

"Money management" is a broad and all-encompassing term, and one that includes concepts like investing and budgeting. To manage a billion-dollar hedge fund requires a high level of skill (or so I assume, as I've never done it myself), but the basics of money management are not difficult, and learning the basics will significantly improve your financial life.

In my experience, one of the most common reasons people get into financial trouble is that they completely ignore the fundamentals of money management, or they attempt to run before they walk. Like David.

> David started a new well-paying job. He needed a car to get to his new job, so he financed it. He moved to a new apartment to be closer to work, so he purchased some new furniture and household items with his credit card (which has a 19 percent interest rate, but David hopes to have it paid off within a year). He decided he wanted to invest his money and earn a decent return. He read a book on investing and decided he needed diversification, so he borrowed $5,000 and invested it in a few penny stocks.

David's story is not unusual. We all want to make money, and we assume that the sooner we get started with investing, the better. We also assume that the more complicated our strategy is (many stocks, not just one or two mutual funds) and the riskier it is (penny stocks, not blue chips), the more money we will make.

Nope.

Starting with the basics is almost always the best strategy. In David's case, borrowing $5,000 to invest in penny stocks makes no sense, because he is increasing his debt. He is paying 19 percent interest on his credit card, and he is borrowing more to invest. That's a lot of debt. David's biggest mistake is jumping ahead to trying to grow his wealth through investing before learning about, and taking care of, the basics of money management.

So what is the answer to David's dilemma? Start with the basics. He would be much better off focusing his time and energy on fundamentals such as the following (all of which we will address later in this chapter), and only then dipping his toe into the investing pool:

- **Reducing debt:** We've already learned that paying off debt is a critical first step to financial health.
- **Minimizing expenses:** Cutting back on how much you spend every month and every year will free up more of your money to get out of debt more quickly, enabling you to save and invest once you do.
- **Developing a savings habit:** Putting money away for a rainy day or for personal goals (such as travel, new furniture, buying a car or a house) is key to ensuring financial security and gaining financial freedom.
- **Enhancing financial literacy:** Learning as much as you can about how to manage your money, even if you rely on advisors to assist you, can enhance your financial well-being.

The answer for David, and for the rest of us, in all areas of money management, is to understand the work of famed Italian economist Vilfredo Pareto.

The 80/20 Rule of Money Management

The Pareto Principle, also known as the 80/20 Rule, states that, for most things in life, 80 percent of the benefit is derived from 20 percent of the cost or effort. Grasping this concept will greatly improve, and simplify, your life.

In many businesses, for example:

- 80 percent of the profit is generated by 20 percent of the products
- 80 percent of the revenue is generated by 20 percent of the customers

Of course, this is not a law of physics and so it does not apply precisely, but it is more accurate than it may initially appear. Test it. If you run a business, make a list of the profit generated by each of your products (sometimes known as SKUs, or stock-keeping units, the identifiers of distinct products or services for sale). You may be able to eliminate a lot of SKUs and not negatively impact profit. "Firing" your worst customers can also increase profitability.

The 80/20 Rule also applies in many other areas of life. Do you want to get into better physical condition? If so, it is likely that 80 percent of the results you receive from working out will come from 20 percent of your efforts. Don't believe it? Try it. Devote two weeks to a very simple, efficient workout (warm up, then do fifty push-ups, squats, and pull-ups three times a week), and then spend two weeks working out at the gym for two hours every day, five days a week. The extensive gym workouts will probably increase your fitness more than the simple workout, but will the gym workouts be *significantly* more beneficial? Probably not. Eighty percent of the benefit comes from 20 percent of the effort, so do that 20 percent well and don't worry about the rest (unless you really like spending time at the gym or you are a professional athlete, in which case, great; go for it).

So what can David, our stock investor, and the rest of us learn from Vilfredo Pareto? Keep it simple. Eighty percent of the profits will come from only 20 percent of your efforts, so focus on the 20 percent. How? I would suggest the following approach.

Instead of David's approach of borrowing to invest, he should do the opposite: pay down debt, and then save to invest. Perhaps David, a first-time investor with no investing experience, is an investing savant who has an uncanny knack for investing in penny stocks just before they make a new discovery and become a billion-dollar company, but I doubt it. If he pays down his credit cards, he instantly generates a risk-free rate of return of 19 percent, and there is no tax owing on that "profit." It's a no-brainer.

David could spend an hour a day analyzing his stocks and buying and selling, and it is unlikely that he would be able to generate a 19 percent after-tax rate of return. He should take the easy path: pay off his credit card debt. Doing that is a lot less than 20 percent of the effort, and he will save a lot more than he is likely to generate speculating in penny stocks. That's the 80/20 Rule at its finest: paying off credit cards and saving the interest is less than 20 percent of the effort of detailed penny stock analysis, but it will probably generate at least 80 percent of the benefit of a good stock portfolio.

But David really wants to invest—everyone is doing it. Fine. He can create cash to invest by minimizing his monthly expenses. He lives close to work, so does he actually *need* a car or does he just want one? What other steps can David take to reduce expenses to free up cash?

Reducing expenses allows David to start saving money, and those savings can be used for investing. His chances of investing success are much greater if he has no interest costs to cover on the money he borrowed to invest. Even if his stockbroker is willing to grant him "margin" (a loan to invest in stocks, which is generally not available on penny stocks) at a 5 percent interest rate, David must generate more than 5 percent to break even. With no debt, his investments can be profitable even if he only earns a 1 percent return.

With a "pot of cash," David can now take the final step that is specific to investing but also to money management in general: Learn. He should read books, research, go to seminars, listen to podcasts, develop an investing strategy, and test his strategy on paper before investing real money. This is the most likely path to investing success.

When Should You Start Investing?

Once you have taken care of the basics of money management (the 20 percent of effort that will yield 80 percent of your financial well-being)—you've eliminated debt, reduced your expenses as much as possible, started to save some money, and increased your financial literacy—*then* you can move on to investing your money to make the most of what you've got. Although I strongly recommend that you learn and perform the basics of money management on your own (like reducing expenses), investing is more risky and complicated than basic money management. It can easily take up 80 percent of your time and effort and account for only 20 percent of your financial well-being (to put it in terms of the Pareto Principle once again). So, start investing when your basic financial life is in order, you have money to invest, and you have the time and inclination to learn to invest prudently.

Practical Advice: Focus on the Basics

Money management does not have to be difficult. And, unless you have the time and inclination, it is not necessary to devote all of your waking hours to learning all aspects of personal finance and investing. However, you must understand the basics, because if you don't, you will almost certainly wind up in financial trouble and you'll never accumulate enough money to invest. Understanding the fundamentals of money management will also enable you to evaluate the advice of professionals once you start seeking their advice. You may never develop the expertise to determine if Stock A or Stock B is a better investment, but by learning the basics you can at least ask intelligent questions.

Make the 80/20 Rule your best friend. A small amount of focused effort will yield big benefits. Ask for advice from successful people you trust. Read a few books. Bookmark some good websites. Part of challenging conventional wisdom is to look out for yourself and ask intelligent questions. By doing this, you'll have a better chance of avoiding the most common financial mistakes and of making decisions that are right for you.

[Myth #17]

BUDGETING IS ESSENTIAL FOR FINANCIAL SUCCESS

*A budget is both a scorecard (to show you your past
successes and errors) and a road map for the future.
If you don't write down what you spend, you can't
see where you are going, so a budget is essential to
financial success.*

Conventional Wisdom

Budgeting Is a Waste of Time

Virtually every financial professional in the world shares the same
opinion: a personal budget is the foundation of any financial plan,
and the preparation of a personal budget is the first step in taking
control of your money. I disagree. For most people, I think budgeting
is a waste of their time. There is a better way to manage money, but

before I explain why budgeting is a waste of time, let's examine what budgeting is and why it is so ingrained in conventional wisdom.

A budget can take many forms, but at its most basic level, it is simply a list of numbers. It is a list of the money you bring in each month and the money that goes out. A budget can be created on something as simple as a piece of paper, or it can be done using a fancy spreadsheet, smartphone app, or computer program that automatically produces fancy graphs and charts.

The need to create a budget is long-established conventional wisdom, for many reasons.

A Budget Forces You to Analyze Your Spending

First, preparing a budget forces you to look at the numbers. In my experience, many people with financial problems have no idea what they spend each month. They know what rent costs because that's the same number each month, but if you ask them what they spend on groceries, or gas for the car, or coffee at the coffee shop, they can only guess.

A budget solves that problem. By recording every dollar you spend, you can look back at the end of the month and see exactly how much you spent on everything. This is valuable information, because it allows you to make conscious choices about where your money is spent.

I once met a lady who spent $400 per month on magazines but didn't realize it because she subscribed to a few of them and picked up others at the checkout counter when she bought groceries or shopped at the drugstore. After tracking her spending for a month, she was horrified that she was spending more on magazines than she spent on gas for her car. So she took action. She decided to make a trip to the library twice a week to read magazines instead of buying them. Boom. Problem solved.

You may think that's an extreme example, and it is (although it is a true story), but what are you spending money on that you don't realize? Do you know exactly what you spent on fast food last week?

Do you know what your hydro bill was two months ago? If you don't know the numbers, you can't make adjustments to your spending patterns, and this is why every financial planner recommends a personal budget. If your goal is to save $400 per month for retirement, where can you find the money? Only your budget knows.

I meet with people and ask them to walk me through their numbers. I grab a pen and a piece of paper, and I ask them what they spend on rent, food, transportation, entertainment, and "everything else." Then I ask them how much they get paid each month. I do the math, and I say, "There's a problem. Based on these numbers, you should have $500 left over each month." But then, as we probe further, and capture all of the expenses they initially forgot, the picture becomes clearer. They forgot about that birthday present they bought for their son last month, or the cost of their daughter's hockey camp, or that unexpected car repair. When all expenses are included, it's obvious that they are short each month. If they were keeping a budget and tracking their spending they would know all of their numbers, and they wouldn't need me to help with the analysis.

A Budget Helps You Set Goals

The experts tell you that a budget is necessary for setting goals and for making a plan to achieve those goals.

We all have goals. Maybe you want to buy a house, or retire, or go on a vacation, or put your kid through school. Those are big goals, and it takes time to save up the money to achieve them. Say I need another $10,000 for the down payment on the house I want to buy. How long will it take me to save the money? If I can save $1,000 per month I'll be done in ten months, but at $100 per month I'll need one hundred months. What is realistic? Only the budget knows.

By tracking my expenses, I can decide to cut back on eating out or on vacations or on something else in order to free up money for my long-term goals. I can then estimate how long it will take to reach my goal, and this will help motivate me to achieve my goal.

A budget forces you to make choices. Do I go out for lunch today, or do I save money and "brown bag" it? Do I take the family far away on an airplane for our vacation, or should we stay closer to home and go on a driving vacation? Without a budget, the experts say, you can't plan for the future, because you don't have the numbers available to make those important choices.

Why Is Budgeting a Bad Idea?

So, if a budget helps you analyze your existing spending and make changes to allow you to reach your goals, why do I think budgeting is a bad idea? Simple: budgets don't work.

Making a budget is similar to counting calories or going on a diet. Did you ever hear the story of that person who went on a diet, lost some weight, but later gained it all back, and more? That's because diets don't work. If you ask the average guy on the street to define the word "diet," he will say something like, "A diet is when you stop eating a bunch of stuff, for a temporary period of time, to lose weight."

A medical doctor or nutritionist would disagree with that definition. They would say that a diet is what we customarily eat, but that's not the definition the average person would understand. To most of us, a diet is a list of "don'ts." I don't eat bread, or meat, or sugar, or whatever. Fortunately, in this view, a diet is temporary, so once I achieve my objective (to lose weight), I can end the diet.

Diets don't work because they are both restrictive and temporary. A restriction is a negative concept, so if you focus on the negatives (what you can't eat), you will eventually give up. According to a random search I did on the Internet (so you know it's true), 95 percent of people who lose weight on a diet gain the weight back within one to five years.

So what do you do if you want to lose weight? I have no idea. I'm not a doctor or a nutritionist, but if I had to guess, I would suggest that you fill your house with healthy foods, stop buying bad foods, and go from there. In other words, you change your lifestyle permanently instead of attempting a short-term diet.

Budgeting is conceptually the same as dieting. In my experience, for many people it becomes a temporary activity to achieve a specific goal. You start out with the best intentions, but a few weeks or months later, you have given up. Take Jane, for example:

> Jane has a lot of debt, and she knows she could cut some of her expenses, so she decides to make a budget. She carries a notebook, and every day she writes down everything she buys and she saves all of the receipts. At the end of the day she records each expense on a budgeting spreadsheet, and on the weekend she analyzes her spending to see where she can cut expenses.
>
> It went great the first week, but in week two, Jane got busy and didn't have time to summarize her expenses. By week three she was behind on recording her expenses and got discouraged because it would take too much time to catch up, so she gave up.

Jane's story is typical. We start out with the best of intentions, but at some point we give up. The number-one reason budgets fail is because **budgeting is difficult**. It's difficult to record every expense and to summarize and analyze every dollar you spend.

How to Not Budget

So, what's the solution? Simple: don't budget. But how can I manage my money and plan for the future if I don't budget? Simple: pay your bills as often as you get paid. That's it.

If you get paid every week, automatically program your bills to be paid every week. If your phone bill is $100 per month, instead of doing what your bill says and paying it on the twenty-first of each month, set up an automatic payment at your bank for $25 every week, on payday. If your pay is directly deposited into your bank account every Friday, set your payment date for every Friday. Simple.

Follow the same process for all of your other living expenses. On Friday you get paid, and when you check your bank account on Saturday, whatever money you have left is what you can spend until your next payday. Simple. If you get paid every two weeks, or twice a month, you modify the system to match your pay schedule. Instead of paying $25 toward the phone bill every week, you pay $50 every two weeks.

This system works great for bills you can pay electronically, but what do you do about bills that you can pay only once per month, like car insurance or rent? You may be surprised to discover that you actually can pay those bills weekly. Talk to your car insurance company and your landlord and ask. If not, there is another choice, and that is to use a separate bank account for bill paying. If my landlord wants only checks, and he wants them only on the first of the month, no problem. I set up a separate checking account, and every week I transfer my rent money into that account. If my rent is $1,000 per month, I have my bank automatically transfer $250 every week from my main bank account to my bill-paying checking account. In my mind, the money is gone. My landlord can cash the check on the first of the month because the money will be there.

Isn't it complicated and expensive to have two separate bank accounts? No. It's not complicated because you don't have to pay much attention to your "bill paying" bank account (and, as discussed in Myth #5, there are some very good reasons for having more than one bank account). You transfer the money and forget about it. Having a second bank account isn't expensive if you shop around. In Canada, there are at least two large online banks that offer free bank accounts, so your bank fees are the same whether you have one bank account or two, or ten.

I remember one of my clients had twenty different bank accounts. She had them at an online bank, so they didn't cost anything. She could access them online or with a debit card. Each payday she transferred money for each expense into the applicable bank account. She had a bank account for groceries, another one for haircuts, one for gas for her car, one for rent, one for car insurance—one for every expense. As an accountant, I was impressed by her attention to detail, but even I think twenty accounts is too many; however, it worked for her.

This is a system where you "set it and forget it." You review your hydro bills for the last year, for example, and make your best estimate of what your bills will be for the coming year. If you are on an equal-billing plan, it's easy. Then you program in your payments, and it's done. Every month you take a quick look at your hydro bill to make sure the balance was paid in full last month, and off you go.

What About Saving Money?

One of the points of budgeting is to save money, and building an emergency fund is a strategy every financial planner recommends. So how do you do that if you don't have a budget? Simple. You program your savings, just like you program your hydro bill. If you want to contribute $100 per month to your RRSP, or TFSA, or RESP, or savings account, no problem. Set up an automatic payment of $25 per week, or $50 every two weeks, so that again you are matching your pay periods.

"But how much should I save?" you ask. "I don't have a budget to tell me how much I should set aside each month." You don't need a budget. You've got something even better: your bank account. Once your bills are paid on payday, you can see how much remains the next day. That's the amount you have to live on for a week (if you get paid weekly), and for savings. You probably won't need much to live on for the week because all of your bills are already paid. You could even have a separate bank account for groceries and weekly transportation expenses so that whatever is left in your main bank account is a good approximation of what you can afford to save.

I define "savings" as any money you are setting aside for the future, with the future defined as "any time after this month." Obviously, traditional savings like a retirement account would qualify, but there is another category where savings are necessary: non-monthly expenses, such as gifts for your family on birthdays and special holidays.

What Day Is Christmas This Year?

Once a year you buy Christmas gifts and once a year you buy a birthday present for each of your children, your spouse, your parents, and perhaps some close friends or relatives. News flash: all of those dates happen on the same date each year. Christmas is always December 25, and birthdays don't change.[1] So why is everyone short of cash after Christmas? How did we not know it was coming?

We knew, but we didn't plan. The budget brigade will tell you to set aside money in your budget each month for once-a-year expenses. That's a good plan, but you don't need a budget to do it. A bank account works fine for that purpose. You can either use your bill-paying account or set up a separate bank account (at an online bank or a bank with low or zero service charges). It will become your "Future" savings account. Every payday you will transfer the appropriate amount into your Future account. How do you calculate the correct amount? Do the math.

Every year, on my birthday, I am required to renew my driver's license and the plates on my car. Let's assume this costs $120 per year. If I just paid my fees for this year, I have one full year to save $120. That's $10 per month, or $5 twice a month. If my birthday is only six months away, I need to save twice the amount ($20 per month). Determine what Future bills you will have (remember, these are the once- or twice-a-year expenses, not the bills you have to pay every single month in the future), what they will cost, and how many months you have to save for them, and that's the amount to transfer each month.

Here's a list of expenses you don't pay every month but that you should set aside funds for each payday:

- Christmas, and every other annual holiday where you spend money

---

1. *unless you are a leap-year baby, but let's not overly complicate a simple concept, okay?*

- Insurance, if paid annually (car, house, life); if you can pay monthly or more frequently, that's easier
- Birthdays
- Vacations
- Back-to-school supplies for the kids
- Car license plates, driver's license
- Dentist or orthodontist
- Other medical expenses

A final word on Christmas and other annual holidays: do the math. Sit down (with your spouse, if you have one), right now, and decide what you will spend on Christmas this year. Christmas is not just the cost of gifts. You should estimate all costs, including:

- Gifts: Make a list of each person you will buy gifts for, and your budget for each person.
- Food: If Thanksgiving or Christmas dinner is at your house this year, what will it cost for the turkey and all the trimmings, including drinks?
- Travel: If you are flying to Grandma's house this year, what will plane tickets and other travel expenses cost?
- Everything else: Your new clothes for the office Christmas party, New Year's Eve party with your friends, and all other expenses during the holiday season.

If you add up all of these expenses and they total $2,400, you need to save $200 per month. If there are only six months until Christmas, you need to save $400 per month, or $100 per week.

If you follow this system, you will have a Future bank account, and each payday you will transfer a not-insignificant amount of money to this bank account. How do you know what the money in your Future bank account is set aside for? Keep a list. The list will look something like this:

- Christmas: spend $2,400 by December 25, saving $200 per month
- Son's birthday: spend $400 on March 15, saving $50 per month

For each Future expense, you calculate the total you will spend and then divide it by the number of paydays that you will be saving for it between now and then.

The Secret Benefit of Not Budgeting

The not-budgeting system is simple and, unlike a diet, it's easy to stick to because you set it and forget it, but that's not the best part. The biggest advantage of the not-budgeting system is that you are saving money, and you don't even know it. I'm not referring to the money you're setting aside for savings; obviously you know you are saving money in your savings account. I'm referring to additional savings you may build up when you plan to pay your hydro bill and all your other monthly expenses this way. Allow me to explain.

In our previous example, your hydro bill is $100 per month, and because you get paid weekly, you transfer $25 each week to your bill-paying bank account. If you are a mathematically inclined reader, you will have noticed that the math doesn't work. Your hydro bill is $100 per month, or $1,200 per year, and you transfer $25 each week to your bill-paying account. There are fifty-two weeks in the year, so you actually transfer $25 x 52 = $1,300 each year. You have overpaid your hydro bill. Why? Because there are four months of the year that have five paydays, so in those extra-pay months you are transferring an extra $25 and, therefore, by the end of a year you have overpaid by $100. The math works exactly the same if you pay bi-weekly. You pay $50 bi-weekly to hydro, or $50 x 26 = $1,300 per year. You have again overpaid by $100.

This is not a flaw in the program. This overpayment is the not-budgeting system's biggest advantage. You "saved" $100 and didn't even know you were doing it. Imagine what it would be like to get a phone call from the collections guy at the hydro company like this: "Hey, dude, you overpaid us by $100; what's the story?" Wouldn't that be a great phone call to get? That's a lot more fun than the "You are behind and we are shutting off your hydro" phone call.

What should you do with this extra $100 payment? You have a few choices. First, you could do nothing and let it accumulate. It's likely that your hydro bill will go up over time, so the extra you are paying will cover the increase in your hydro bill, at least for a while, so you can keep paying the same weekly amount and stay on track.

Second, you could adjust your payment. Instead of paying $25 per week, you could pay $23.08 per week, which, when multiplied by fifty-two weeks, ends up as $1,200 per year. Although personally, I don't like this idea, because I am prejudiced against decimal points and because you aren't taking advantage of the hidden savings in the not-budgeting system.

Third, you could take a payment holiday once a year. Perhaps in February, during RRSP season, you could stop putting money aside for hydro for a month, or two or three weeks, and instead send that money to your RRSP. Your cash flow would be the same each week, but you will have squeezed a few extra dollars into savings or investments. Alternatively, you could use the extra money to make a lump-sum payment on your debt, or you could increase the amount in your Future bank account. It's up to you. Take advantage of it. You earned it.

But I Like to Budget

Then fine, make a budget. I'm a chartered accountant, or what we now call a Chartered Professional Accountant. So I get it. I like numbers; I like spreadsheets; I like graphs and charts. If that's the way your brain works, go for it. If you enjoy crunching the numbers and watching your savings grow, great.

Like I said earlier in this chapter, my objection to budgeting for the average person is that they won't stick to it and they will get discouraged and stop, which is worse than doing nothing at all. Diets are the same for the average person. You get started with the best of intentions, but it's difficult and you don't stick to it, and then you go on an eating binge and end up twenty pounds heavier than when you started your diet. Similarly, if you try to budget and fail, you get discouraged, you stop looking at your credit card statements, and you may end up more in debt than when you started. That's why I like the not-budgeting system.

The One Example Where a Budget Is Not a Waste of Time

Now that I have convinced you that budgets are a bad idea, let me give you one example where I have seen success with budgeting for many of my clients in real life. This may be mere semantics, but for some people keeping a spending journal may help them save money.[1] What's the difference between a budget and a spending journal? Not much, other than perspective.

A budget is *forward looking*: it's a list detailing how I plan to spend my money over the next few months. A spending journal is *backward looking*: it's a list of what I already spent today, and in the past. A successful budget combines both elements. You have two columns for each month: budget and actual. You record what you plan to spend, and then record what you actually spent.

I said that budgeting is a waste of time, because it's difficult to keep track of what you spend. But if you actually do it, it can save you money. Some people go on a diet and count calories and lose weight. Doesn't that prove that diets (and budgets) can work? Yes, that's true. It is certainly possible to lose weight by counting calories. Even if you continue to eat exactly the same foods and

---

1. Gail Vaz-Oxlade explains how to integrate a budget and spending journal on her blog gailvazoxlade.com/blog/archives/5341 and in her book Debt-Free Forever, www.gailvazoxlade.com/resources.html

get the same amount of exercise, the act of counting calories may be enough to help you lose weight. You know that you will have to write down that cookie in your food log, which forces you to think about eating that cookie, and so you don't eat the cookie *so you don't have to write it down!*

For some people, the concept is the same with a spending journal. The knowledge that I will have to record that purchase in my spending journal may cause me to change my behavior and not purchase that item. I know the purchase is unnecessary and I know it will "look bad" in my spending journal, and because I don't want to look bad (or make myself feel bad), I don't make the purchase.

A spending journal makes you conscious of your spending decisions, just as counting calories makes you conscious of your food intake. Being aware of your actions makes you change your actions, because we are all emotional creatures. A spending journal may allow you to "trick" your emotions into working for you, not against you, and if that system works for you, go for it.

Practical Advice: The Perfect Budgeting System

So what am I saying? You should budget, or you shouldn't? A spending journal is a good idea, or it isn't? What I'm saying is this: If you like budgeting, budget. If you don't have the time or inclination to budget, develop your own "non-budgeting" money management system, or combine elements of both to create a system that works for you. The key point is that you need a *system*. You want a system that makes it simple to accomplish your goals.

If I'm not a morning person and I'm always late for work, but I want to be on time for work so I don't get fired, I need a system. The system may be to lay my clothes out the night before and set the timer on the coffee machine the night before so that in the morning I can get out of the house quicker and make it to work on time. That's a system.

If I want to lose weight, I can count calories, which will help me be more conscious of what I eat, but that's not a system; it's an action that I take, and it works only if I keep performing that action. A better system would be to get rid of all of the junk food in my house and fill my kitchen with healthy foods, so I have no choice but to eat good foods. That's a good system.

If I want to control my spending, I need a system. For some people, maintaining a budget works. If you want to track your spending, do it. If you like budgeting, do it. The fact that you enjoy it greatly increases your chances of success. You are almost guaranteed to be successful. Go for it. But for many people budgeting is difficult, so they need a better system. Setting up automatic payments is a good system because you are not required to make a decision about how to spend your money. If you have only healthy food at home, you don't have to decide whether or not to eat junk food while watching TV at night. If your spending is automatic, you don't have to decide how to spend your money. That's a good system.

There's no reason you can't combine my not-budgeting system with conventional budgeting. You can set up all of your expenses using automatic payments each payday and then use a budget to track everything, making adjustments as required. That may be the perfect system. The trick is to know yourself and what motivates you so that you can pick or design a money management system that will work for you.

[Myth #18]

I AM IMMORTAL

*In the event of your untimely demise, as long as you
have life insurance you have provided for your family,
so you don't need to worry about anything else.*

Conventional Wisdom

There Is More to Death than Life Insurance

Unless scientists figure out the secret to immortality, you will die
someday. You know this. Intellectually, you believe this. But you don't
act like you believe this, you act like you will live forever. You disagree with that last sentence. You protest and say, "That's ridiculous."
But your actions don't jive with your words. Like with Armando.

Armando loves his wife and two children. He is a good father and
a good provider. He takes his son, Ricky, to hockey practice every
Saturday morning at 5:00 am. He takes his daughter, Susie, to hockey
practice every Sunday morning at 6:00 am. His wife, Maria, works late

two nights a week and on those nights Armando, while not a great cook, barbeques hotdogs and hamburgers for the kids.

Armando's got a great system to pay the bills each month. The bills get delivered to him electronically, he reviews them, then he sets up the payments on the day they are due through his online banking. Easy. He has life insurance through work (equivalent to one year of his salary) and he has life insurance through the bank to insure the mortgage. He has set up RESPs for the kids. He's got it all covered.

Armando is a truck driver, so he frequently switches jobs, always for higher pay. Then, one day, the unthinkable happens. Driving home from work, Armando gets side-swiped by a truck, and he's gone.

Shortly after Armando's death, his life insurance through the bank is activated and it pays off the mortgage. Unfortunately though, Armando started a new job just two months before his death, and his employee benefits, including life insurance, were not due to start until the end of his three-month probationary period. Therefore, Armando had no company life insurance at the time of his death.

Maria and the children do their best to carry on. And life goes on, until three months later, when Maria starts getting phone calls from the hydro company, and the gas company, and the phone company, and a few others. Apparently the monthly bills are not being paid. Maria doesn't know what to do. Armando used to handle all of that.

Maria doesn't have access to Armando's bank account, so she doesn't have a list of all of his "Bill Payees" or the account numbers for the bills. What bills need to be paid? She doesn't know. Even worse, she has no life insurance money and the family no longer gets Armando's paycheck, so cash is now very tight.

According to conventional wisdom, Armando did everything right. He had a will, and he had life insurance. Unfortunately though, his life insurance through work ended when he changed jobs, and the new policy hadn't kicked in yet, so at the time of his death he had no company life insurance. As a result, Maria did not receive any money to help the family pay the bills.

You, like Armando, are not immortal, so you need to plan for your inevitable death.

I know, as emotional beings we don't like to think about death. It is not a pleasant subject. If we were rational entities, thinking about death would be no big deal, but we are not rational. Death is an emotionally charged concept, so our rational brains shut down whenever we are forced to consider the idea.

The first step is to recognize that you and I, quite naturally, have an emotional response to death. The trick is to channel your emotions positively, and the way to do that is to think not about your death but instead consider the plight of your survivors. I'm an accountant, so I recommend channeling your emotions in a positive manner by using a checklist.

The Death Checklist

No worries, I've got you covered with my handy-dandy death checklist. Follow these steps and you can die tomorrow. Your family will be very saddened by your untimely passing, but because you will have left everything in good order they will have a great funeral for you, you will be remembered fondly, and they won't have to worry about their financial future.

1. Cover the basics

The conventional wisdom that started this chapter is incomplete: you cannot base your entire estate plan on life insurance alone and adequately provide for your family. However, life insurance is important and it does serve as a good starting point.

Life Insurance

Here's the question: if you die tomorrow, can your family survive financially without you? If your income pays the mortgage, your death will seriously impact your family's cash flow. If you have debt, ditto.

So you need to consider the various types of insurance and their associated cost, and then make some decisions.

The least-expensive life insurance, in most cases, is term insurance. With term insurance there is no investment component; your estate only gets paid if you die. It's similar to car insurance: you pay, and if you have no claims, at the end of the year your money is gone, and you pay again. (With whole life insurance, some of your premiums are invested, but the cost is much greater.) Buying term insurance to pay off your mortgage in the event of your death is often a good "investment," as without a mortgage payment your family will not need as much to survive after your death.

■ PRO TIP: get a quote from both your insurance agent and your bank, and go with the least-expensive option. Banks often charge higher fees on life insurance than an independent agent.

Whether or not you need more than just mortgage life insurance is up to you. If you have life insurance through work and you aren't concerned about losing your job, you may have sufficient coverage. If your job is unstable, you may need more. Again, the question is simple: "If I die tomorrow, what happens to my family?" If you have lots of cash in the bank and no debt, life insurance is less of a concern than it should be if you have a lot of debt and your family has no other sources of income.

Will

If you have assets in your name, you need a will so that those assets can be distributed the way you want them to be when you die. If you have no assets, there's nothing to distribute, so a will is less critical. Again, at the risk of stating the obvious, the time to make a will is *before* you die, so do it now.

You can make a will yourself by simply writing out your wishes on a piece of paper, but there are pitfalls to this method, so I don't recommend it. If you expect to have any assets when you die, or any final requests, it is prudent to enlist the services of a competent lawyer to draft your will to make sure that it is valid (do-it-yourself wills often are not), and because a lawyer will know what issues may arise after your passing. You don't want an ambiguously word-ed will to lead to family disputes once you are gone, and that's why the services of a good lawyer now may eliminate many disputes in the future.

The first issue to be addressed in your will is your assets. If you have a spouse and three children, for example, who gets what? Typically you would leave everything to your spouse, and vice ver-sa, unless your spouse predeceases you, in which case you would probably want to leave your estate to be divided equally among your children. Probably, but not necessarily. You could leave your antique car to your daughter who collects antique cars, and you could leave your small business to your other daughter who founded it with you. You can do whatever you wish, but you should think about it now, and then have the lawyer record your wishes in proper legalese.

Another key thing to consider and include in your will is, if you have minor children, what happens to them? Do you establish a trust for them? Do you appoint a guardian until they reach a certain age? These are tricky questions, and best left to a lawyer to draft a will that accurately reflects your wishes.

Finally, your will should be updated as your circumstances change. For instance, if you divorce and remarry, it is likely that you will want to amend your will to leave your assets to Spouse #2, not Spouse #1, although that, too, is a decision for you to make.

Power of Attorney for Personal Care

If you become incapacitated, in most jurisdictions your spouse can make medical decisions for you. However, if you are single, or an eighteen-year-old kid going off to university who doesn't have a spouse, then a medical power of attorney, or a "living will," may be very important. Again, this is relatively simple for a lawyer to draft, and it can save considerable grief.

A Power of Attorney for Personal Care, often also called a Medical Power of Attorney, allows a person to whom you appoint the power to make personal care decisions on your behalf in the event that you are unable to. For example, you can specifically direct that medical treatment should be discontinued so that you can die naturally if there is no reasonable expectation that treatment will assure your recovery from your physical ailments. In other words, you can specifically request that your "attorney," or personal representative, authorize the doctors to "pull the plug." Or not. You decide. You may decide that you want specific interventions (nutritional feedings, artificial mechanical respiration) and don't want others (electrical or mechanical heart resuscitation). The point is that you should think about your wishes now, have an appropriate Power of Attorney for Personal Care drafted, and then communicate your wishes to your loved ones so that there are no surprises.

Power of Attorney for Property

While your lawyer is at it, have him or her prepare a Power of Attorney for Property as well. If you are dead, your will describes how to deal with your property. If you are incapacitated but not dead, your Power of Attorney for Property will contain your instructions regarding your property.

For example, if you are injured in an accident and in a coma, what should happen to your house? If you are in a coma, who will pay the mortgage? Is there money to pay the mortgage? Or should the house be sold? What about your car? Stocks? Debts? Your spouse will presumably be perfectly capable of dealing with your assets, but without a Power of Attorney for Property, your spouse does not have the legal authority to deal with assets that are in your name. You don't want to leave your spouse responsible for the upkeep on a house that he or she doesn't have the power to sell or remortgage.

Again, these are difficult issues to consider, but it's far better to do it now, and discuss it now, than leave it for the future when you may be unable to do so.

2. Get your spouse in the loop

This is key: Armando thought he was sparing his wife a burden by paying the bills every month, and he was—until he wasn't.

In every family I have ever met there is a "division of duties." One spouse will typically do more of the cooking than the other. One spouse is more likely to do more of the housework than the other. One spouse often handles the finances. A division of duties is not a bad thing (as long as it's fair), and it's actually smart to have one person to handle the monthly bills. If two of you are trying to keep track of when the hydro bill is due, for example, it's likely that you will sometimes either miss it or pay it twice. So having one spouse pay the bills make sense; it's a mechanical exercise that can be done by either person; however, both spouses must be "in the loop." Both must know the basics, such as:

- How do the bills arrive each month? By mail? E-mail? Via electronic banking?
- How do the bills get paid each month? By pre-authorized payment? Via online banking?
- How do you access the bank account to pay the bills?

That last point is the key one. Do you both know the log-in name and password to all the bank accounts you have, together and separately? If Maria knew Armando's log-in name and password, or if she had her own log-in name and password for each of the joint accounts, she would have had easy access to his funds and to all the bill payment information, so she could have easily paid all of the bills.

The bottom line is, life insurance on its own isn't enough. You both need to be in the loop about all your financial matters.

The "In the Loop" Checklist

I'll make it simple for you. Fill out the list below and give a copy to your spouse. In fact, your spouse may have some of the information needed to complete this checklist so, better yet, fill it out together. Then each of you should save an electronic copy in a password-protected file, so that either of you can immediately take over the family finances if needed.

Bonus tip: This list is useful only if the information is kept current, so every time you open a new bank account or change a password, create a new list and send it to your spouse (and vice versa). It would be prudent to review the list at regular intervals, perhaps twice a year, to ensure that the information is current. Pick two days for your review and send yourself a postdated e-mail to remind you to do your semi-annual review. Good days to pick would include New Year's Day or one or both of your birthdays (because they don't change each year), or a day in the middle of the year (like Canada Day or the Fourth of July).

Here's the list:

- **Bank accounts**: For each account, list the bank name, bank account number, online-banking website address, log-in name, log-in password, and answers to any security questions (if applicable).
- **Investment accounts**: This will include retirement accounts, the company stock plan, and any other investments. Your list should include all details necessary to liquidate the investments (provided they are covered by your will or Power of Attorney for Property) and include the name of the financial institution where the investments are held, the contact name of the financial advisor (if applicable), the type of account (RRSP, TFSA, etc.), account number, and log-in information (if applicable).

- **Regular monthly bills**: This will include account numbers and payment methods (automatic withdrawal, check, Internet banking, etc.) for normal monthly bills like hydro, gas, phone, cable, Internet, etc. You don't want to find out that your hydro was shut off because you didn't pay your bill.
- **Irregular bills**: These are bills you don't pay every month, which may include your annual payments for car, house, and life insurance.
- **Contact list**: What plumber do you use? Electrician? Guy who fixes the pool? If you have this information but your spouse doesn't, write it down.
- **Other stuff**: This is a "catch all" category for everything else. Do you have a manual for the water softener? A warranty for the lawn mower? Make sure your survivors know your filing system.

■ **PRO TIP:** After you make your list, go through your online bank and credit card statements for the last year to check if there are any other bills you may have forgotten to include, and add them to the list.

Making a list is a hassle, but once you do, you will have protected your family, and that's a good feeling.

Practical Advice: Information Is Power . . . and Insurance for Your Family

This entire chapter consists of practical advice, but the most practical consideration is this: focus on protecting your family. This chapter is not really about legal paperwork (wills, powers of attorney, and checklists), although that's part of it. What your family requires in the event of your untimely passing is information, so your focus should be on anticipating whatever information your heirs may require and providing it to them well in advance of the date on which they will really need it.

[Myth #19]

PAY YOURSELF FIRST

*To build wealth, pay yourself first. If you wait to save
money until the end of the month, you won't have any
money left, so always pay yourself first.*

Conventional Wisdom

Saving Isn't Always the Best Strategy

This basic rule, pay yourself first, makes perfect sense. Every financial advisor will tell you, "The first bill you pay each month should
be to yourself." The reason is simple. If you have ten bucks in your
pocket, it's difficult to resist buying an extra snack on your way
home from work. If you have no cash in your pocket, you won't be
tempted. Simple.

I agree with the basic premise that we should determine our
priorities before making decisions. If I decide that my number-one
priority is to get up early and go to the gym, I can arrange my life to
achieve that goal. I can go to bed early, not go out drinking late at
night, and I can arrange my work schedule to accommodate.

Money management is the same. If I decide that my priority is to save for retirement or my children's education or whatever else, then I should arrange my finances to achieve those goals. Paying myself first seems like a logical way to accomplish those objectives. However, paying yourself first works only if saving money is indeed your number-one priority. For many people today, it isn't.

For many people, their primary goal should be the elimination of debt and saving should be secondary. If you have student loans, pay them off. If you have high-interest credit cards, pay them off. In these cases, your rule should not be "pay yourself first"; it should be "pay off your debts first." Paying interest on a credit card at 20 percent so that you have money to invest in a savings account at 1 percent is ridiculous. Pay your debt first.

But I Want to Establish a Savings Habit

Yes, I've heard that argument. Saving is a habit, the experts say, so you should start saving immediately to establish the habit, even if it's a small amount. The experts would tell you that if you have $100 extra each month, you should use some of it to pay down debt, but be sure to put something, even $10, into savings each month to establish the habit.

Nonsense.

I agree with the concept of establishing a habit, but the experts miss the point. The habit is not "saving money"; the habit is making a plan to prioritize your expenditures.

Practical Advice: Adopt Good Financial Habits

Make a list of your debts, with the highest interest, callable debts at the top of the list (see Myth #8), and set a target for the amount that you will pay down on those debts each month. Then, with each paycheck you earn, pay them down. That's a good habit. The habit starts with deciding on your priority, making a plan to achieve it, and then doing it. Whether it's a debt-repayment goal or a savings goal is irrelevant. What matters is the process.

Your goal is not having savings. That's the end result. Your goal is to adopt good financial habits or a good *process* or *system* for managing your money. This will allow you to work toward paying off your debts (the first habit) and then you can start a savings habit, which may be followed by an investing habit. That's a good system.

Now, of course, if you have no debt, paying yourself first makes perfect sense. But only if you have no debt. Simple.

[Myth #20]

JOINT BANK ACCOUNTS
ARE ESSENTIAL
FOR COUPLES

*Some say you should have a joint bank account
with your spouse or partner to make paying the
bills easier. Others advise that you should have
separate bank accounts because if you ever get
separated you want to have access to your own money.
Which is the right thing to do?*

Inconsistent Conventional Wisdom

Should You (or Shouldn't You) Have a Joint Bank Account?

In every other chapter of this tome we have examined conventional wisdom and explained why it is incorrect. In the case of whether or not you should have a joint bank account, there is no consistent conventional wisdom.

A financial planner will tell you that you and your spouse should have a joint bank account, for two reasons:

1. You will pay less in bank service charges if you have one bank account instead of two or more. If your bank charges a base fee for a bank account, you want to pay that fee only once.

2. It's easier to keep track of transactions in one bank account than it is when you have more than one account.

I agree with the financial planner's second point. I have worked with many couples over the years where he pays some of the bills and she pays others, and they each have their paycheck go into their own individual account, so they both have to keep track of who is paying what, and when. One joint account would simplify their money management process.

Divorce lawyers, on the other hand, will tell you to maintain separate bank accounts. In fact, they will tell you to keep everything separate: bank accounts, investment and retirement accounts, real estate, and all other assets. That way, if you separate, you, and only you, have access to your money.

So who is correct? Should you have joint accounts, or not? The answer is: yes. In other words, you should have a joint bank account to transact your joint business, and you should have separate accounts for non-joint activities. Simple.

If you, as a couple, are able to agree on your basic money objectives, a joint bank account is the way to go. (If you are not able to agree on your basic objectives, either work together to figure it out or stop being a couple.) As a couple, you have shared expenses, and those are the expenses that should be paid from your joint bank account. Obvious examples of shared expenses would include rent or mortgage payments, utilities, insurance, transportation, and other living expenses. Examples of items that are not shared would include items that cannot be shared, like individual retirement accounts. They can be in your name only, so they are not joint.

When It Makes Sense to Have a Non-Joint Account

There are two logical reasons to have your own bank account.

Reason #1: Deposit insurance requirements. In Canada, the Canada Deposit Insurance Corporation (CDIC) insures bank deposits up to a maximum of $100,000 per person, per institution. So, if you and your spouse have $120,000 in a bank account or term deposit at a bank, it is not fully insured. However, if each of you has your own account with $60,000 in it, all of the money in both of those accounts is fully insured. Having separate accounts makes sense.

Reason #2: For your own protection. There are numerous situations whereby your joint bank account becomes inaccessible, including:

- A service disruption at your main bank, in which case having a second bank account at another bank allows you easy access to cash.
- The death of your spouse. With a joint bank account you can continue to access the account because it is also in your name (but at some point the deceased's name is removed from the account, so having your own second account may, again, make it easier to access cash in an emergency situation).
- If your spouse experiences financial problems.
- If you become separated or divorced.

Those final two points require further elaboration. Let's explore using an example.

Lloyd and Melanie have a joint bank account. Lloyd is self-employed and got behind on his taxes, so the government froze all of his assets, including his joint bank account. Unfortunately, Melanie's pay is deposited into the couple's joint bank account, and so once their account was frozen she had no access to money to buy groceries or pay any bills.

It's not fun having money in a bank account that you can't access. That's why, if either partner is at risk of experiencing any financial problems, separate bank accounts are essential. My advice for Melanie would be to have her own bank account, solely in her name, and perhaps even at a separate bank for added protection. Her pay should be deposited into her bank account.

How should Melanie handle their monthly living expenses? If one partner is in serious financial trouble, the obvious solution is for the other partner to pay all bills from his or her sole account. In this case, if Lloyd has any income, he can deposit it into Melanie's account, and then from there she can pay the mortgage and other living expenses. With this approach, if Lloyd's bank account is frozen, it's not a big deal, because there won't be much, if any, money in Lloyd's bank account and they will still be able to access money and pay bills.

■ **PRO TIP:** If you are self-employed or in any way at risk of being sued, you should own nothing. The spouse who is not at risk of being sued (because he or she is an employee and not in financial trouble) should own the assets. In this case, Melanie should own the family home and have the bank account from which the bills are paid. Lloyd can own his business, but that's it.

Of course, it's not as simple as transferring all of the assets to Melanie's name at the first sign of trouble. If the house gets transferred to Melanie's name on Monday and Lloyd goes bankrupt on Tuesday, Melanie has a problem; the Licensed Insolvency Trustee administering Lloyd's bankruptcy estate will overturn that transaction. If there is a mortgage on the property, the mortgage lender must agree to any transfer of assets, so transferring assets into one spouse's name may not always be possible, but it should be considered.

So, if you are going into business for yourself, transfer all family assets to the non–self-employed spouse before you are in financial trouble, and in that way you are protected.

To summarize: If there is no chance that either partner will have creditors attempting to seize assets, a joint bank account is the simplest way to keep track of your money. Keep it simple. There is nothing simpler than just one account. However, if you have a lot of wealth, having separate accounts spreads the risk and allows you to qualify for more deposit insurance at your bank.

If one of the partners is self-employed (which increases the risk of legal action), separate bank accounts are prudent. Separate accounts for borrowing, including credit cards and lines of credit, are also prudent to allow both partners to build their credit ratings. If only one partner has all assets and liabilities in their name and they die or there is a separation, the other partner is starting from scratch. That's a problem.

So, review your situation and pick the options that work best for you and your partner.

Why Is This an Issue?

Why do we even need to consider something as simple as joint bank accounts? It's an issue, because it's an emotional issue. The conventional wisdom is that merging our finances when we get married is a sign of our commitment to each other, and that having separate bank accounts indicates we aren't fully committed to the relationship. Perhaps, but as I have argued throughout this book, it is important to recognize the emotional aspects of all decisions, and to do your best to remove the emotional elements from the decision.

If you have trust issues with your partner, having separate bank accounts may be a problem, but that's an emotional problem, not a financial problem. Deal with the underlying emotional issues first, so that you can make the correct financial decision. The best sign of a commitment to each other is mutually reviewing all of your options and making the decision that is best for your family.

Practical Advice: Look Out for Yourself

Evaluate your own unique situation. If you are in a relationship now but believe that there is a chance that you will be single in the future, it is prudent to have a bank account and probably a credit card or other form of credit in your name exclusively. Even if you are in a solid relationship, the unexpected death of your partner (see Myth #18) would make you single, so having separate banking facilities is prudent.

If you are in a solid relationship, doing most of your banking through a joint bank account is generally the simplest, least-expensive approach, but analyze your situation and do what is best for you and your spouse.

[Myth #21]

YOU SHOULD ALWAYS HELP YOUR FAMILY AND FRIENDS

If you have the ability to help your family, you should.
You should loan your friends and family money,
because if you can't help those closest to you, who can
you help?

Conventional Wisdom

Never Loan Money to Family or Friends

Thinking of loaning money to family or friends? Don't do it. Ever.
Let's consider the story of Mabel:

Mabel is a widow, sixty-five years old, with three adult children. She
is a really good person. She is kind and giving, and never complains
or asks for anything for herself. Her son, Randy, went through some
tough times. He lost his job and then went through a divorce. He

needed a place to live, so he moved back in with Mabel for a while and she loaned him money for lawyer's fees for his divorce, and she loaned him money to take care of some of his debts and for first and last month's rent for a place of his own. Mabel is on a pension and doesn't have a lot of money herself, so she borrowed against her line of credit to get the money for her son. He promised he would pay her back, but he still hasn't found a good job, and now Mabel is maxed out on her line of credit and is having trouble covering her own rent and her debt payments.

Sadly, this is a very common story. I have met with many "Mabels" over the years, and they are all good people, wanting to do the right thing. Unfortunately, if you borrow money to help someone and they can't repay you, you can end up in serious financial trouble, and you may even need to go bankrupt yourself.

I have genuine empathy for people like Mabel, because she was honestly trying to help, with no regard for her personal situation. I assume that her son, Randy, was also genuinely thankful for her help and had every intention of repaying his debt in full. Unfortunately, life happens, and when Randy was unable to pay back the money, Mabel was left in a very precarious financial position.

In my experience, this is most common with seniors. "Once a parent, always a parent," as the saying goes, and it is difficult for mothers and fathers to view their offspring as anything other than their children, because that's what they are. We are genetically programmed to help and protect our children, which is great for the preservation of the human species when the children are young, but is of less value when the child is forty years old. It's difficult for parents who have always helped their children to say "no" to their requests for financial assistance.

I have one strong recommendation: Never loan money to family or friends. Why? Because in addition to the potentially negative financial ramifications, if they are unable to repay you, you may also lose a friend or suffer irreparable harm to your family relationships.

Thanksgiving dinner isn't a lot of fun if the topic of conversation is, "When are you going to pay me back that money I loaned you?"

How to Say No (or Yes)

So what should you do if a friend or family member asks for financial help? Here's my strategy: First, and most importantly, you should determine what help you can actually afford to provide. If you have a million dollars in the bank and your son asks for $50 to fix the flat tire on his car, you will not suffer any adverse financial consequences if you accede to your son's request. However, if you are like Mabel, on a fixed income, and the only way you can help is to put yourself into debt, you should seriously consider whether or not you want to jeopardize your financial future to help your adult child. If you can't help, say so.

I can think of many people who had to file bankruptcy because of the debt they incurred to help their adult children. They just couldn't say no. When they finally went bankrupt and lost all access to credit, they had one profound feeling: relief. They could honestly tell their children, "Sorry, I would love to help you, but I have no credit and no money, so it's impossible for me to raise the cash to help you." Not having the money is the perfect excuse for not helping, because it's the truth.

My point is that you don't have to wait until you file bankruptcy to say no. You don't owe anyone an explanation, but if you feel compelled to give one, tell the truth: "I don't have the financial resources to lend you money. I can't put myself into debt, and jeopardize my retirement, to help you out. I can't."

What if you are financially stable, and you can help out without jeopardizing your financial future? The next question to ask is: "Should I help?" At some point, we all must "grow up" and fend for ourselves. If you continually bail out your friends and family, they will have no incentive to take care of themselves by reducing their living expenses, getting a better job, and working hard. Think of it this way: Are you helping a gambling addict by giving them money to gamble? Are you helping a person with a drinking problem by buying them a drink? Should you offer a match to someone who is trying to quit smoking? So why would you help someone with a spending or saving problem continue to live beyond their means? Sometimes the best help you can give is no help at all.

But what if the person genuinely needs your help? What if your daughter is going through a separation and needs a place to live until she can get back to supporting herself? What if your son has a medical issue and requires medication, and he can't afford it? If you decide that you have the resources to help out, and that person really needs your help, my advice is the same: don't loan them money. However, if you feel so inclined, *give* them the money. No strings attached, no conditions, no expectation of repayment.

Why a gift and not a loan? Because there is no legal or moral obligation to repay a gift. The recipient does not have to feel that they are indebted to you. (They may feel that way, but it's not a legal obligation.) You don't have to worry about whether or not you will ever be repaid, because there is nothing to repay; it was a gift.

So if you have the money, and if they really need it, give it to them. If they say they want to pay you back, say, "Fine, but don't even think about it until you are back on your feet."

House Loans

But what about loaning your children money for the down payment on a house? Isn't that a good idea? What's wrong with parents helping their offspring get a good start in life? Again, there are two questions to ask: "Can I afford it; and am I actually helping or harming my kid?"

Larry bought his first house thirty years ago, and in total he's owned four houses; every one of them went up in value. He wanted his adult children also to benefit from home ownership, so he gave his oldest son $50,000 toward a down payment, and he planned to give his two daughters a similar amount when they finished university and were ready to buy a house or condo. Larry's son split up with his wife, and she got the house as part of the separation agreement; Larry's down payment was gone. Larry had some business issues of his own and was unable to help his daughters when they were ready to buy; they now resent the fact that their older brother got money from Dad, and they probably won't.

This may sound like a fanciful, made-up story, but it isn't. It's very common.

As a parent, you have an additional decision to make: will I help all of my children equally? If your family is like every other family in the world, each child is different. They have different jobs and different earning capacities. Some are married, some are not. Some want to settle down and buy a house; some prefer to be mobile and rent.

If you are the parent, it's your money, so you can loan or give it to your kids as you see fit. But, if Kid #1 gets money and Kid #2 doesn't, will that create friction? Will Thanksgiving dinner be uncomfortable? Is that what you want? Let me repeat my advice again: don't loan your kids money.

Now you get it. You understand why it's dangerous to loan your kids money, but you want to help, regardless of what I say. Since you won't take my advice, here's what you should do if you really want to help them out.

First, think of all of your children together. Kid #1 needs help today, but Kid #2 may need help tomorrow, so don't spend all of your money on Kid #1 and have nothing left for Kid #2. Second, do the math and determine what you can afford to give them, **on the assumption that they will never pay you back.** Third, let all of the kids know what the deal is.

The deal may be, "Kid #1 needs help, the rest of you are fine on your own, so I'm only going to help Kid #1." It's your money, you can do that. Or the deal may be, "I have $300,000 in investments that I probably won't need and that will probably form the basis for your inheritance when I die, so I'm going to set aside $100,000 for each of my three kids, and I will give them that money when they are ready to buy a house, or start a business, or go to school, or whatever other suitable purpose they may have for it. It will be a gift, not a loan."

While personally I believe we should all learn to fend for ourselves, it's your money, and you can distribute it as you see fit.

What About a Second Mortgage?

Instead of gifting the money to my child, should I loan them the money to buy the house and secure it with a second mortgage? Yes and no.

If Larry had lent his son the money and secured it with a mortgage, when his son got divorced Larry would still have had a claim on the house, so in the separation there would have been less equity to distribute between Larry's son and his ex-wife. That's why a second mortgage is a good idea: it protects the lender in the event of a marriage breakup or if the borrower must declare bankruptcy; the equity, up to the value of the mortgage, goes to the mortgage lender, not the other creditors.

However, loaning money to a child to buy a house may complicate the process of them getting a first mortgage. It may be necessary to tell the bank you "gifted" the money so your child qualifies for a mortgage; in this case, you can't register your second mortgage until the financing is in place for the first mortgage. Also be aware that it costs money to register a mortgage and you must agree on repayment terms, if any.

Let me emphasize again the two salient questions: can you afford it, and are you helping your kid? If you can afford to lose the money, whether it's a gift or a second mortgage is less important. Of more importance is whether you are truly helping your kid by loaning or gifting them the money to buy a house.

I can tell you many stories of parents who provided the money for a down payment, and as a result the kid bought a house much bigger than he or she could reasonably afford, which caused severe financial pressure for the kid, because the cost of a house is more than just the cost of the mortgage. It's great that Mom and Dad helped with the down payment, but they probably won't be helping with the utilities, property taxes, or repairs and maintenance, so by "helping" Junior buy a house, they may, in fact, have subjected the poor kid to many years of being trapped in a house he can ill afford.

The issue is that the future is uncertain. Your child doesn't expect to lose her job or get divorced, and she doesn't expect that the real estate market will ever decline, but stuff happens. The best answer in times of trouble may be to sell the house, reduce expenses, and rent for a period of time until the situation improves. However, if I'm the child and selling the house means I won't be able to fully repay my parent's loan, I may decide to hold on to the house until I'm back above water. I feel obligated to repay my parents, so I continue to own when I should be selling. The house becomes an anchor, holding me in place when I need to move. I'm trapped.

If house prices go up and Junior gets a promotion at work and has a long and successful marriage, your second mortgage will be repaid, with interest, and everyone will live happily ever after. That would be great. However, if Junior gets transferred to another city and must sell the house quickly, at a loss, and is not able to fully repay your loan, you have a problem. If Junior gets divorced or loses his job or if the real estate market corrects, Junior may not be able to repay your loan in full. Now Junior feels bad, you are upset, and the other kids are worried that you won't be able to help when they need your assistance.

The Bailout

There is a final category of assistance that I see all too often: The bailout.

> Amanda's parents gave her a 5 percent down payment so she could buy
> a house. The maintenance costs were more than Amanda expected,

but she managed by using her line of credit to pay the bills. Then
Amanda lost her job and got behind on her mortgage, so her parents
gave her the money to catch up on the mortgage, but they didn't have
enough money to help her catch up on the property taxes, and when
the basement flooded Amanda didn't have the money to make the
repairs, so she ended up selling the house at a loss. She was not able to
repay her parents for the down payment or any of the bail-out money.

Again, this is a very common story. It is not uncommon to help someone pay their debts, only to see them lose the house anyway. Buying
a house with 5 percent down is a recipe for disaster. If the real estate
commissions will be 5 percent when you sell the house, you have no
equity, so no margin for error. You can't afford any surprises, like a
leaky roof or flooded basement.

When you are that close to the edge, spending more to cover extra costs is usually throwing good money after bad. It was probably
inevitable that Amanda would lose the house, so her parents did her
no favors by delaying the inevitable. She should have sold the house
sooner, and that would have saved her parents a lot of money, and
grief.

Beware of the conventional wisdom that advises you to take care
of family and friends above all else; think about how helping them
out financially might affect them and your relationship. As much as
you love them and think you're doing the right thing by helping them,
consider the future carefully before financially assisting friends and
family.

Practical Advice: The "Helping Family" Checklist

The simple solution is don't loan anyone any money. If you really
want to help, give them a gift with no expectation of repayment, and
before you do anything, answer these questions:

1. **Can I afford to help**? This question is critical. If you will need to borrow to help your family, you can't afford it. The answer is no.

2. **Will helping help**? Giving your kid the money for a 5 percent down payment to buy a house they can't afford is harming, not helping. At best you are enabling bad financial decision-making, and at worst you are setting them up for a financial disaster. Don't do it.

3. **If I decide to help, how can I protect myself**? Registering a second mortgage after loaning the money may protect you if the house must be sold, but if your child divorces or can't make the payments, you may still incur some costs to collect your money.

I know of many families who have been irreparably harmed by "helping out," and that's why, if possible, I suggest you avoid it. Loaning money to family is an emotionally charged activity; it is very difficult to loan money to family in a rational manner, but as with all money decisions, it helps to focus on the practical, rational aspects before deciding to make the loan.

My final piece of advice: think about Thanksgiving or Christmas, or whatever the next family gathering will be. Will your financial help bring everyone closer together, or cause more stress?

It's your money, so it's your decision.

[Myth #22]

LIFE IS LIKE A BOX OF CHOCOLATES

Mama always said life was like a box of chocolates.
You never know what you're gonna get.

Forrest Gump

Life Isn't Always Sweet . . . But It Is Predictable

Is Forrest Gump correct? Is life an uncertain mystery, where you never know what will happen next? In some ways, yes. You don't know that a distracted driver will rear-end you on the way home from work tomorrow, causing damage to your car and whiplash to your neck. You don't know what the car repairs will cost, and how much rehab you will need before your neck functions normally.

Perhaps life is completely random, but let me advance an alternate hypothesis: life is completely predictable. It's true that if you close your eyes and grab a chocolate from the box, you don't know whether you will get the kind you like or that gross kind you hate.

But who actually does that? Not me. Most chocolate boxes have a cheat sheet, with pictures of each kind of chocolate and a description of their contents, so I check the sheet and then grab the kind I want. There is no uncertainty at all. But what about my car that broke down yesterday? No one could have predicted that!

I agree that it is impossible to predict the exact moment that you will get a flat tire, or that the "check engine light" will light up on your dashboard. But I can predict that, since you are driving a twenty-year-old car and you haven't had an oil or tire change in three years, it is very likely that one of your bald tires will go flat and your engine will seize up due to the lack of lubricant. I can't predict the exact timing, but the outcome is 100 percent certain.

"But what about that time I lost my job?" you ask. I understand. I have helped thousands of people who experienced unexpected job loss, but here's a prediction for you: You will not be working at your current job fifty years from now. At some point, you will no longer have the job you have now. You may retire, or find a better job, or get fired, or the company may close down. I don't know the exact timing, but I know the end result: you will not have your job forever.

I'm a Licensed Insolvency Trustee, so I help people who have too much debt. Guess when my phone rings a lot. Go ahead, guess.

I'll tell you: it hardly rings at all in mid-to-late December, but then on January 2 it starts to ring, and the number of phone calls continues to increase through the winter and into the spring. Why? Because at Christmas everyone is spending money and not worrying about their debts. After the New Year's hangover has subsided, people log in to their online banking and are shocked at the credit card balances. They call me, and continue to call me all the way through to the end of tax season in April, and beyond. Every year Christmas is a surprise, it seems.

Let me make another prediction, and you can quote me on this one: Christmas will be on December 25 this year. I guarantee it. Most of the other days where you spend a lot of money are also easily predictable. Tax time is the same time every year. Birthdays, when you buy presents for your kids and family members, are exactly the same day every year. Summer vacation? It's always in the summer. Always.

We humans focus on today, which presumably is a survival instinct from the times when we had to focus on finding food and shelter and avoiding the lions any given day, because if we didn't survive today, tomorrow didn't matter. But in the modern world we live in, it is likely that if you are alive today you will be alive tomorrow, and it's highly likely that you will be alive ten years from now, so our bias toward today should be moderated by a thought for tomorrow.

Planning for tomorrow has two components: money, and everything else.

The Money Plan

The money plan is conceptually very simple:

1. Make a list of all of the days that you know will mean you'll be spending money: Christmas, birthdays, vacations, the day your license sticker on your car comes up for renewal (which is probably your birthday), and so on. Decide what you will spend on each of those days, and start setting aside the money for it now. (Chapter 17 on how *not* to make a budget will give you more guidance on this.)

2. Make a list of all of the events that you know will happen but you don't know exactly when: car repairs, house maintenance (like when your appliances break), and start setting aside the money for those events.

I realize it is impossible to estimate precisely the cost and the timing of every possible future event, but the basics are not that complicated.

By consciously thinking about the future, you can plan for it, and not be surprised on January 2 when the Christmas bills hit your mailbox.

The "Everything Else" Plan

A money plan is important, but so is the "everything that isn't money" plan. Start by looking for your next job, even if you have a great job that you expect to be at for the rest of your working life. Why? Because nothing lasts forever.

I can tell you hundreds of stories of people who were shocked when they lost their job, but in hindsight they should have realized that it was likely to happen, because there were lots of warning signs. Companies don't go out of business in a day; a decline takes time. The common warning signs, which are often obvious only in hindsight if you don't know what to look out for, are things like the inability to replenish inventory, a lack of new orders, changes to upper management, and no new hiring. If these events are happening at your employer, the "writing is on the wall."

So how should you prepare for a potential loss of employment?

- **Always be networking**: Keep your eyes open. Stay "top of mind" with potential employers and influencers in your industry. What would you do if you lost your job tomorrow? Do that, starting today.

- **Build your personal brand**: Are you primarily identified as an employee? Is your Twitter handle @JoeABC_Company? If it is, do you lose all of your social media capital when you leave your job? My Twitter handle is @doughoyes, which will work great regardless of where I work or what I do in life. By all means, help your employer; it's a good way to get a raise and keep your job. But don't forget to build your personal brand at the same time.

The "Everything Else" Plan should include strategies for dealing with any reasonably predictable future event. Some examples:

- If your landlord sells your house, do you have a strategy to find a new place to live? For some people this is easy: you just find another place. But if you have a pet, or you don't have a car so you need a place close to work, or you need a wheelchair-accessible apartment, it may be prudent to "keep your eyes open" in the event that you need to move quickly.

- If you have a medical issue, do you have a plan? We discussed the importance of life insurance in Myth #18, but what about medical insurance? Are you covered at work? If so, what are you covered for? Can you get coverage if you lose your job? If you currently have coverage, this is not an issue; but it's wise to have a plan in the event that your situation changes.

- If your car requires major repairs, can you get to work? This is different than the "plan for unexpected expenses" issue. If you have savings you can pay for car repairs, but if you drive your car through standing water and it fries your engine and it will take three weeks to repair it (don't ask me how I know it takes three weeks; just trust me on this one), do you have a back-up transportation plan? What if tomorrow morning you discover your car has a flat tire or a dead battery? Having a friend you occasionally carpool with may be good insurance. Joining CAA may also be prudent.

The point is that stuff happens, so think about it now, and make a plan.

Practical Advice: Prepare for the Inevitable

In simple terms, plan like a pessimist but live like an optimist. For example, you probably won't lose your job tomorrow, so don't walk around with a cloud over your head. However, you may want to, or need to, switch jobs in the future, so plan ahead.

In fact, with a plan, life can actually be sweeter than you may expect. Not all surprises are good, so instead of closing your eyes and blindly grabbing the first confection you touch in the chocolate box of life, scan the possibilities, give some thought to what you want out of life—and go for it.

POSTSCRIPT

It must be true. I read it on the Internet.

Conventional Wisdom

Just Because It's in a Book Doesn't Make It True

The purpose of this book is not to tell you what to think. I have shared my opinions; however, given that I am an emotional, fallible human being, it is likely that some of my conclusions are wrong or might even be a disaster if applied to your own unique situation. This is the case with any book. You shouldn't blindly follow the opinion of any author.

The same is true, if not exponentially more so, when it comes to information that can be found online. We live in the age of Facebook. (Although I don't . . . I find Facebook a bit creepy. So, while I have an account for business purposes, I don't check my personal page, which is why I have a bunch of unanswered friend requests. Don't be offended. I'm not ignoring you—I'm ignoring everyone. But I digress.)

On social media, everyone is an expert. For example, when my team posts a story on our Hoyes Michalos Facebook page, it is inevitable that someone will immediately post a comment disagreeing with what we posted and will offer an alternate opinion, often in less-than-polite language—which is another common occurrence on social media: people get emotional. They use exclamation points and emoticons in an attempt to sway your opinion at an emotional level, particularly when they are lacking actual credentials to be providing advice on a given topic. That's just how it works.

So how do you know who to trust? How do you know if @BigGuy79359 on Twitter is a credible source of information on which you can rely to make decisions affecting your financial future? How do you know if conventional wisdom exists because it is true or merely because no one has questioned it yet? The answer is: you don't know if @BigGuy79359 is credible and you don't know if what you read on Facebook, or in any book, is good advice in your unique situation.

You must start by recognizing that emotion plays a role in almost all decisions we make and that a reliance solely on emotions may not lead to the correct decision. You must determine the relevant facts, consider all alternatives, crunch the numbers, and attempt to make a rational decision. You must think. The good news is, you can, and you will.

You want what is best for you and your family. You want financial success. If you are not currently as successful as you want to be at making good financial decisions, is it all your fault? No. The biggest Canadian bank spends over three-quarters of a billion dollars each year on advertising, and with that advertising onslaught, it's not surprising that it's difficult to resist the conventional wisdom being propagated by banks that debt is good.

Sometimes a bad decision is not your fault, but you already know that. You know that the car salesperson is an expert at putting you in the most expensive car they can, and you know that the job of a real estate agent is to sell you a house whether you can afford it or not. I understand. That's why I wrote this book.

We have a common enemy. Our enemy is not the big banks, or the car salesperson, or the real estate agent. They have a job to do, and they, like all good persuaders, will appeal to your emotions to make a sale. Our enemy is an irrational decision-making process, whereby we don't take the time to consider the facts but instead rely on our emotions to make the final decision.

By recognizing how you have resorted to often-inaccurate conventional wisdom to make decisions in the past, you can achieve financial success by pausing and thinking first. You can own a car, buy a house, pay for college, and have a care-free retirement. Whatever your goals are, you can achieve them by understanding that the most successful people don't blindly follow conventional wisdom, and that is why they are successful.

Here's to your success.

Additional Resources

Hoyes, Michalos & Associates Inc.

Ted Michalos and I founded Hoyes, Michalos & Associates Inc. in 1999 to help ordinary Canadians solve their debt problems. We offer bankruptcy and consumer proposal services to those who struggle with the burden of overwhelming debts. We take pride in helping people who are experiencing financial hardship find a successful way out of debt.

Over the years of providing debt relief services we've heard almost every creditor, professional advisor, and debtor story you can imagine. In this book, I've chosen to share our knowledge and experience on how to solve your money problems.

As we have learned from the preceding chapters, information is key to improving your financial situation. Rather than relying on the conventional wisdom of family and friends, and even the financial industry, it's critical to do your own research. To get you started, here are some additional resources we provide:

- Go to hoyes.com—our website contains hundreds of helpful articles.
- Check out our *Debt Free in 30* podcast on iTunes and other podcasting apps.
- Watch the Hoyes Michalos YouTube channel, which features over 100 videos.

Use your judgment and apply what you read, listen to, and watch as appropriate to the facts of your situation.

Knowledge is power in most things, and that's especially true when it comes to your financial health. I can't emphasize enough: do your research.

www.hoyes.com

Contact Us

Straight Talk on Your Money is available for bulk purchase. It makes a great gift for clients and partners, and is an excellent promotional item for your organization.

Please contact us for more information and discounts available.

Contact: Doug Hoyes
Phone: 519-568-4185 or toll free 1-844-790-9289
Email: doughoyes@hoyes.com
Twitter: @doughoyes

ABOUT THE AUTHOR

Doug Hoyes, BA, CA, CPA, CBV, CIRP, LIT, is the co-founder of Hoyes, Michalos & Associates Inc., one of Canada's largest personal insolvency firms. In his thirty-year career as a chartered accountant and Licensed Insolvency Trustee, he has personally helped over 10,000 individuals solve their debt problems and rebuild their financial future.

He has appeared before the Senate Banking, Trade and Commerce Committee in Ottawa to give testimony on the impact of bankruptcy legislation on the individual, and serves as an OSB (Office of the Superintendent of Bankruptcy) Oral Board Examiner.

Doug is a passionate advocate for ensuring that people find the right solutions for their debt problems. Frequently interviewed in the media, he has shared his knowledge and expertise on the most common financial mistakes and traps on *Global News*, CBC, *The Globe and Mail*, the *Toronto Star*, Business News Network, *The Financial Post*, and *CTV News*. He posts regularly to the Hoyes, Michalos blog, to Twitter (@doughoyes), and on Huffington Post Canada.